THE Silent DEATH

Juliet Sesanker-Daniel

THE SILENT DEATH

All Scripture quotations are taken from the Holy Bible, King James Version, which is in the public domain.

ISBN-13: 978-1-926676-61-6

Printed by Word Alive Press
131 Cordite Road, Winnipeg, MB R3W 1S1
www.wordalivepress.ca

Dedication

I would like to dedicate this book to our Lord Jesus Christ, who chose me to write it for Him. Ten years ago in a dream, the Lord showed me this book. I saw the title of the book, I saw the design of the book, and I saw my name on the cover of the book. I asked the Lord, why, why did I have to write this book? He said, "So that millions of people will be saved."

I thank God. I thank You, Holy Spirit, for writing *The Silent Death* for me. Without Your help, I could not have done it. I give You all the praise.

To the Father, the Son, and the Holy Spirit I give You all the glory, the praise, and the honour for this book. I pray that whoever reads it will hear Your voice and I pray that this book will accomplish that which You sent it to accomplish. I love you, Lord, I praise You, and I honour You.

Acknowledgements

I want to thank my husband Andy, my children Kristin and Gregory, my sister Claudette Guy, my brother Horace Wilson, and my cousin Rev. Colbert Sesanker, who encouraged me to complete this awesome task.

I want to say a special thanks to my pastor, Pastor Evans Barning, and his wife, Pastor Vida Barning, for all their prayers, advice, and encouragement. I would also like to thank Sister Claudia Hamilton, Sister Ann-Marie Junor, Sister Pauline Wright, Sister Leela Sinanan, and Sister Louise Monney for their research, their prayers, and for their encouragement.

I cannot forget to mention two of my past students, Vladimir Toptchi and Valentine Bona, who from the onset of my dream, kept asking, "When is your book going to be finished?" To them I say, thanks for the encouragement.

Foreword

When I started this book ten years ago, I did not know exactly what the Lord wanted me to write about. I wrote about my experiences in life, but somehow I felt that my memoirs were not what the Lord wanted me to write, so for a few years I left the book in a drawer, not willing to pick it up. Then one day, at my church, there was a visiting pastor who told us to pray that night and ask God to visit us.

That night, the Holy Spirit visited me. It wasn't until after His visitation that I knew exactly what had to be written in *The Silent Death*. The Holy Spirit gave me the headings for every chapter in this book and I depended on the Holy Spirit to write this book for me. Thank you, Holy Spirit!

Whether you are a Christian or not, *The Silent Death* is a book which you should read with an open heart. It will help you understand that dying does not only mean a physical death, but that it can also mean spiritually and emotionally.

Many of us go through life not reaching our God-given potential, not knowing what God's plans are for our lives, and we just live on anyhow, accepting all the negative things that come our way. This book will teach you ways in which you can die without knowing that you are dying and it will teach you the ways in which to escape the silent death.

All the Biblical quotes are taken from the King James Version and please note that the advice given in this book is given directly to me from the Holy Spirit. May God help us in defeating satan's plans for our lives.

In this book, satan's name will always be lowercased, even when starting a sentence, because he was cast out of Heaven into Hell; he was brought lower than the angels. We should not dignify his name by capitalizing it. God is more powerful than satan. satan's name should not be glorified, hence the reason I decided to write his name in lowercase throughout this book.

Those wishing to contact the author please e-mail: julietsesankerdaniel@gmail.com

Table of Contents

Introduction

Many women have high self-esteem. They take pride in who they are. They love. They care for others. They possess great talent and have much wisdom and knowledge to offer. However, before they know it, these things are ripped from their grasp. I am referring to women who, from their youth, have given so much of themselves, only to be violated by others, leaving them helpless and hopeless. They are tossed out like yesterday's garbage.

How does this violation occur? As teenaged girls, boys overwhelm their thoughts. Nothing else matters at this time in their lives. Mind you, I am speaking from my own experience and observations. In today's society, girls are more exposed and experienced than one could ever imagine. Today it is becoming more prevalent for thirteen-year-old girls to engage in sexual activities that would have been considered taboo twenty years ago. Many of us see our teenaged daughters going down a path that we know will ultimately lead to destruction. But what do we do? What can we do?

While many of us mothers profess to have all the answers, the truth of the matter is that we are helpless. We really do not know what to do or where to turn. We hide behind a mask, because we fear that our so-called friends and family will know the truth about what we are going through. We fear that people will say mean things behind our backs, and we fear being embarrassed among our peers.

However, I am here to tell you that there is nothing to be embarrassed about. There is nothing to be afraid of, neither is there anything to be despondent about, for the Bible tells us that God is always with us. He is our teacher, our provider, our helper, and our friend. Today I am writing to tell you that satan is here to destroy our teenagers, our youth, our young adults, and even the older men and women in our society. You may ask, "How do you know that satan is here to destroy our young girls and boys in our society?" I know because he started with me, and over the past forty years I have seen his pattern in my life and in the lives of many men and women around the world.

This book is about the many ways satan robs boys and girls and the techniques he uses to kill and destroy the men and women in our society. On a daily basis, young girls and women are being robbed of their virginity, their love, their minds, their emotions, and their inner souls, all because of naivety and lust.

To all the teenagers, youth, men, and women reading this book, what I am about to discuss will finally open your eyes to some valuable truths about our lives. Many of you may have experienced the wrath of satan in the form of brothers, sisters, mothers, fathers, friends, lovers, husbands, wives, teachers, colleagues, bosses, prayer partners, ministers, neighbours, and confidants. Personally, I have been tried and tested. However, I have proven that satan is a liar, a thief, a destroyer, and a killer, which is what led me to write this book, *The Silent Death*.

Although many of you are bearing wounds from your past, I am here to tell you that Jesus Christ is Lord, and that because of

Jesus there is a way out, a route of escape. There is victory to be experienced, whether you are a teenager, a young adult, or an older man or woman. God has a plan for your lives no matter where you have been, no matter what you have done, and no matter where you think you want to go. From this moment on, God Almighty has a plan and purpose for your life, but you must first believe in Him and you must accept Jesus Christ as your Lord and Saviour.

The Lord Jesus Christ is there for us all. He stands with us at all times. We simply need to live for Him and ask Him to direct our path and to be in control of our lives daily. I promise you that you will have the victory if you give Jesus free and full reign in your lives.

Teenagers, young adults, men, and women, listen up: the following chapters may reflect what some of you are going through at this present moment, what some of you have already experienced, or what some of you will experience. I am sharing my story in an effort to help you avoid satan's traps, his lies, and his path of destruction. I promise you, if you take heed to what the Holy Spirit is telling you, you will not be living a silent death. Instead, you will be living a victorious life!

1
My Experiences

I was born in Tobago, the sister island of Trinidad. I have a twin sister named Claudette. Although we are twins, she is somewhat opposite to me. Our differences were quite evident in our adolescent years. The things she liked, I hated. She liked bright colors; I liked earth tones. She was on the chubby side, and I was slim, which might explain why I was more outgoing and she was more reserved. Her reserved nature was a blessing for her, because at the tender age of sixteen she accepted Jesus Christ as her Lord and Saviour. I, on the other hand, was a rebel and did things to please myself.

I always knew I wanted to be a teacher, but at fifteen, doing well academically was not a priority. I was more interested in having a boyfriend. There were other boys interested in me, but when Tim said he wanted to go out with me, I was elated. The same young man, who had not even acknowledged my presence for an entire year, finally spoke to me and asked me to be his girl-friend. Of course, I said yes!

Tim was tall and handsome. All the girls liked him and wanted to be with him, but they knew that he belonged to me, so they stayed away. Guys, on the other hand, did not stay away from me. They did not care that Tim and I were dating. They still flirted with me and made passes, but to no avail. My heart belonged to Tim.

While Tim and I were dating, Claudette was living for the Lord. She went to the Pentecostal church, gave her heart to the Lord, and was living an upstanding Christian life. I was angry with her lifestyle and ashamed of her. After all, we had been brought up to be good Catholics, so why should she leave our be-lief to join the "poor people's church?" You see, the members were not allowed to wear pants, jewellery, or makeup, all of which I loved to wear, so that was not the place for me.

As a teenager, I had an exciting life. I was on top of the world! I had everything, at least I thought so at the time. I was very attractive, came from a good family, and was dating a hand-some guy from a good family. What more could I ask for?

As I said, I was on top of the world. I was in love, and that was all that mattered. The fact that I was engaging in sinful con-duct did not bother me. I abused my body, my soul, and my spirit. At the time, I did not care that I could have died and gone to Hell. No, none of these things mattered to me—not at fifteen, not at twenty. The only thing that mattered was that I was living the "high life." It was the life of luxury!

In retrospect, I only *thought* I had it all. I thought living for the moment was all that counted. I took no concern for where I would end up, whether I would be educated, or whether having a relationship with God was important or not. I thought I was on my way to Heaven no matter what I did because I faithfully attended the Catholic church and received communion each week.

Please listen to me, teenagers. As a teenager, I made many mistakes. I made mistakes that could have resulted in the loss of my life had it not been for the hand of God being upon me at the time. I was not even aware of it. As I reflect on the mistakes I have made, I think about my daughter Kristin and my son Gregory. I thank God that they both accepted Christ as their personal saviour. Each day, I pray that they will not live the way I did.

MY ADVICE

Teenagers, stay away from alcohol. I drank as a teenager—not frequently, but occasionally. I was what one would call a social drinker. Although I despised the taste of beer, I would drink whenever I went to parties or discos, to be cool, to feel important, and to be accepted by the crowd. I even drove after drinking, knowing that it was wrong. I could have become a statistic. I could have perished, and I would have been destined for Hell. You see, I wanted to be liked by all.

I never drank to the point of getting drunk, though; I always seemed to be able to hold my liquor. Tim, on the other hand, did not drink at all, preferring malt or pop. I don't even know if he knew I drank alcohol. I never drank in front of him. I did not want him to know that his Ms. Perfect had flaws.

This is what some teenagers do. They do things behind their parents' backs, behind their teachers' backs, and behind everyone else's backs so that they can maintain a positive reputation. However, I'd like to tell you that although I hid things from my family, friends, and acquaintances, and although Tim did not know I drank, God knew. God is the one who we cannot hide things from, because He sees all, hears all, and knows all... even before it takes place.

Girls and young women, please, please listen to me. You may think the way I did. You may think that since you will be a teenager only once, you might as well enjoy life. I am not for one moment suggesting that you should not enjoy your youth or your teenaged years. I am simply advising you to accept Jesus Christ as your Lord and Saviour. Allow Him to have full control of your life before it is too late.

Many of you may have started to smoke cigarettes and weed, or you might be doing cocaine or other drugs that are available. Many of you may have already fallen into satan's trap to destroy your life. However, now is your opportunity to turn to Christ, and make some positive life-changing decisions.

To be honest with you, I smoked my first cigarette at twelve years of age. One of my uncles had just died and an older cousin of mine decided to smoke a cigarette to relieve her stress. She asked me if I wanted to try it, and I did. I was not able to conceal what I had done because I started to cough uncontrollably. My mom, Marie, caught me. Although I was not punished for my conduct, I quickly realized that smoking was not for me; it tasted awful, and the smoke prevented me from breathing.

I later tried smoking again when I migrated to Canada at age nineteen. I really wanted to be cool in this new country. I was on a student visa and I partied along with the other girls in the dorm. We partied from Friday night until Sunday. While many of the girls did drugs, I experimented with cigarettes. I hated it, but I smoked anyway, wanting to be a part of the in-crowd. Thank God I did not keep up this habit for long. I managed to quit before it became a habit.

While you may have heard such lectures over and over again, many of you have let it go in one ear and come out the other. Many of you are like me; you just want to be cool, accepted, and a part of the in-crowd. But whose in-crowd do you really want to be a part of? You definitely do not want to be a part of the Lord's in-crowd, definitely not the crowd that wants to see you live a good healthy life, and definitely not the crowd that wants to see you make it into Heaven. Teenagers, it matters what you do to your bodies now. It matters that you take care of yourselves now, and not just in ten, twenty, or thirty years. Now is when life counts, now is when it matters, because one day you will have to answer to God as to why you abused His temple.

Speaking of the abuse of one's body, do you know that when you engage in sexual activity with Tom, Dick, Harry, or Jane, you are abusing your body? Do you know that even if you are sleeping with *one* partner, you are still abusing your body and breaking God's commandments?

Teenagers, please note that it is not a guarantee that you will marry the first person you sleep with, so be careful. Many guys will tell you things like, "I love you, you're the only one for me," just to get you into bed with them. Be aware that this is just a line, for if they really love you, they would wait to marry you first, then have sex after marriage. Nothing in life is a guarantee. There is an exception to that rule—if you accept Jesus Christ as your Lord and Saviour, when you die, you *will* make it into Heaven. This is *guaranteed!*

When you commit the sin of fornication, you can never erase the emotions that come with it. You can never reverse the consequences that follow your actions. Many teenaged girls have ended up pregnant after their first time having sex. Many of them claim that they knew what they were doing, and some even used protection, yet ended up pregnant.

Young ladies, you do not want to use your bodies as a tool for satan. You do not want to get involved in sexual relationships that are just for lust or experimentation. Your bodies are for that special someone, when you are married and are responsible for your emotions, desires, and consequences. Just imagine the joy you and your husband will have knowing that you both waited. Saving your virginity until marriage will eliminate that baggage of soul-tying problems, problems that result from having sex with different partners.

Yes, don't you know that for every man you sleep with you are spiritually tied to that person? Then for every other woman he sleeps with, there are multiple soul ties taking place. Let me explain something to you. When you say you have a soul mate, it simply means that you are connected by your souls, and that you are in sync with each other. So just picture yourself giving yourself to every boy you like, flirt with, or whichever tickles your fancy. What do you imagine is going on when you sleep around with them?

I will tell you what happens when you sleep around with guys, or other girls for that matter. When you sleep with a guy out of wedlock, you lose your self-respect, you lose your dignity, you lose your virtues, and you are tied to that person spiritually. When he goes on to sleep with another girl, he passes your spiritual baggage on to her, and you pass his spiritual baggage on to every other guy that you sleep with. In other words, you are now connected to all these people spiritually.

Take a moment to think about this. Imagine that you and your best friend slept with the same guy, then he goes on to sleep with others, you go on to sleep with others, and your best friend sleeps with others. Think about the chaos this causes in the spiritual realm. Your souls are all connected and there is a struggle to disconnect this rollercoaster of confusion that you have all created. That is why so many young boys and girls are so frustrated with their lives. That is why so many men and women are suicidal, confused, and cannot get out of their oppressive situations in life.

Many young girls who have started having sex at thirteen and fourteen, today as adults do not know what is wrong with their lives. All they know is that although they are married, they have an unhealthy and unhappy relationship with their husbands. They also find that their jobs are not satisfying and that life in general fails to meet their expectations.

Unfortunately, they are unable to pinpoint what the problem is. Some have the best careers, best homes, best husbands, and best children, but deep down inside they are dying. They are confused and they are frustrated with themselves, everyone, and everything around them. Why? They cannot answer this question. Their therapists cannot answer this question. As a matter of fact, no one but God can answer their questions. In fact, the only way one can be released from soul ties is to be delivered. Yes, you must accept Jesus Christ as Lord and Saviour and you must pray for His ultimate deliverance.

You may say, "Well, Juliet, what do you know about this topic?" For years, I have spoken to people about their experiences. I have seen how satan used their bodies to commit the sin of fornication, and I have seen their struggles, their pain, and their sorrow, all of which stemmed from having sex before marriage.

How many of you believe that you can be happier in life? I am not talking about being happier as a result of material things, nor am I talking about winning a lottery to make you happy. I am talking about self-satisfaction, self-motivation, and self-preservation.

For so many of us, we "aim to please." No matter the cost to our health, our strength, or our bodies, so many of us are programmed to please others. Yet, by pleasing others we get sick. The unfortunate thing is that some types of sicknesses do not manifest themselves until years later. Some types of sicknesses are fatal, yet we fail to notice because of our ambition to please!

Some of us think that if we do not please our husbands, our children, our pastors, our neighbours, and friends, we will not be considered good women. Many of us wives extend ourselves beyond our limit in an effort to please others. However, we get nothing in return for our sacrifices. We still get blamed if our kids end up on the wrong side of the tracks, if there is no money in the bank, or when things that we are not responsible for go wrong.

So many preachers say, "Take it to the Lord in prayer," yet some of us have been praying for weeks, months, and maybe even years about our situations. It is not that the Lord did not hear our prayers, and it is not that He did not answer us; it is that sometimes we do not listen and other times we get our wires crossed. By this, I mean that when we want something badly, no matter what God is telling us to do, we do things our own way.

Why is human nature so rebellious? Sometimes we see non-Christians flourishing and we get envious. We ask ourselves, why are they so successful when they aren't serving the Lord? Brothers and sisters, do not be angry or jealous, we do not know what they are doing to acquire their riches. It is important that we continue to pray and wait on the Lord. It is through Christ that we will receive our strength, and our riches.

Recently, a woman won fifteen million dollars in the local lottery here in Toronto. When the newscaster interviewed her with regards to what she was going to do with that money, this is what she replied, "I am going to buy a house in the Bridal Path for me, my four children, and eight grandchildren. The house costs eight million. I am also thinking of buying a Lamborghini, and then I will travel." In my mind, I questioned, why would she do that? Why would she buy a house in one of the richest areas in Toronto? Is she aware of the amount she will have to spend in property taxes? Is she getting a Lamborghini for the purpose of proving to people that she has money, that she is now a millionaire?

I am not saying that I was not happy for the woman. I was very happy for her. I just think her millions will go as easily as they came. Riches are from God; therefore, I am a very rich woman. I do not have large sums of money at this point in my life, but I am very rich. I have a roof over my head. I have a loving husband, two God-sent, loving children, and I am doing what the Lord has asked me to do. I am also an Elementary School Teacher by profession.

Since the Lord placed this book upon my heart in 1999, I have been working at what I wanted to do. After working for years with the federal government and at various banks, I decided to go back to school to become a teacher. This is something that I always wanted to do. I must tell you that throughout my years of teaching, I have been faced with many illnesses. It seems as if God has been trying to get my attention for the purpose of writing this book.

Currently, my condition according to the doctors is called Myofacial Syndrome. This is a type of sickness that causes severe headaches to the left side of my head. I also experience numbness and excruciating pain in my face, neck, and down my left arm. I get tingling sensations in my face and down my left hand as well. I have not worked for over four years, yet the Lord is providing for me. I am telling you this to show you that when God asks you to do something, do it and do not be afraid.

I once thought that I could not write for the Lord. I thought that such a task would be too difficult. Well, the Lord stopped me in my tracks with this illness and now I am at home because I am too ill to return to work as a teacher.

I know that this is the time to write what God has placed on my heart. It's now or never. Mind you, I know I am healed already; it will be God's time to manifest my healing. However, while I wait, I *will* accomplish God's purpose for my life. It is up to Him to determine whichever form or fashion He sees fit to use me. It is all in God's hands.

2
Things That Plague Women

The list of things that plague women is lengthy. It starts with food addictions, weight control, drug and alcohol abuse, low self-esteem, feelings of unworthiness, missed opportunities, regrets, broken promises, and it can end with unfaithful husbands. While the list goes on, I am only going to touch on a few.

"Husbands?" you may say. Yes, they can be the number one culprit. I have spoken to many friends who suffered and struggled in their marriages. In some cases, it made no difference if their husbands were Christians; the Christian wives experienced the same hardships as the non-Christian ones.

The marriage flowed smoothly until the birth of the first child. With the baby came weight that stayed on. Unfortunately, many of these husbands were dissatisfied with their wives' post-baby figures. They made statements like, "Why can't you do something about that belly you're carrying around?" "Why aren't you doing something about the skin tags on your face and the stretch marks on your belly?" From such remarks, the comments escalated to, "Look at you, you look like a fat cow," or "You're looking old, can't you do something about yourself?" Suddenly, they no longer considered their wives to be attractive and they eventually looked elsewhere, because to them, "the grass is greener on the other side."

Another issue worth noting is the consumption of food. Oh yes, some women eat when they are nervous, anxious, bored, depressed, hurt, and angry... and for a whole list of other reasons. I know, for me, I overate as a result of depression. At a certain point in my life, I ate and ate and ate because I felt that I was not good enough. I felt that I was never doing anything right, so every time I felt depressed, I ate.

You see, ladies, negative words can have a harmful effect on you. I think that verbal abuse is worse than being physically abused. I am speaking to and about educated, bright, beautiful women who have struggled to get where they are, yet their husbands condemned them; they stripped them of their dignity and robbed them of their joy, their inner worth, and their pride.

Some husbands use this tactic to keep their wives beneath them. Some use this verbal abuse as a tool to feel good about themselves and to have power over their wives. Ladies, why do we allow these men to control us, to dominate us and to have power over us? While the Bible tells us that the man is the head of the home, it does not give men the permission to abuse their wives verbally and physically.

As women, we should stand up and know that God is for us. Stand up and know that we should not allow our husbands, boyfriends, or anyone to control our lives and strip us of our dignity. We are to decide once and for all that as human beings, this is not what God put us on earth for. We are here to accomplish what He said for us to accomplish, and those that are abusive to us are merely satan's ploy to block us or remove us from our destinies.

To the men reading this book, please be aware that girls, young ladies, and women are sensitive to words. Words hurt, they cut deep wounds into us, potentially leading to depression, addiction, and suicide. Unfortunately, these feelings will not simply go away by giving her a rose on Valentine's Day or a gift on her birthday. These feelings can last a lifetime. Women need to feel wanted, appreciated, loved, cherished, and adored.

No woman wants to feel that she is second best. If you know that you are verbally abusing your wife, please stop, ask God to forgive you, and ask Him to help you to treat her with respect, despite the changes that may have taken place in her physical appearance over the years. Seek professional help if you have to, but stop and stop now. Tomorrow may be too late!

The next issue I would like to mention is that of broken promises. I have heard of and seen many young girls commit their time and energy to support and love boyfriends who promised to marry them. These ladies worked hard, they struggled, and some even paid for their boyfriends' education, only to be rejected by that same boyfriend.

Suddenly, their girlfriends are not good enough. They are not educated or suave enough. What do you think this is doing to women in our society? What do you think goes on in the minds of these women? Personally, I know of some women who never trusted men again. I know of some who went off the deep end and others who remained spinsters till the day they died, all because of men who used them to get ahead in life, then left them after accomplishing their goals. Think about it, men. Would you like another man to treat your sister that way? No, so please don't treat someone's daughter that way!

3
Weight Issues

Put your hand up if you have ever struggled with your weight. I'll be the first to raise my hand. My twin sister Claudette and I have struggled with our weight for years. We were both born small—she was four and a half pounds and I was four pounds at birth. However, throughout our childhood we were quite plump. At age twelve, I started doing yoga stretches from a book, five days per week. Throughout my teen-aged years, I maintained a weight of one hundred and ten pounds on a five foot six body.

I migrated to Canada, got married, had kids, went back to school, worked, discovered certain chocolates, and whammo! I am currently over two hundred pounds. Do not get me wrong, I am not blaming any of the above; I am blaming myself for feeding my emotions, struggles, and problems with food.

While I know exactly what to do to lose this weight, it is a struggle. Although I know the Lord is there to help me, it is as if every time I get one step forward with weight loss, I go two steps backward. I have all the books, all the knowledge, yet I struggle. It is as if I am hiding behind this weight. It is my comforter. You see, having been slim and trim throughout my teenage years, I know what it is like to feel good about myself and what it feels like to be in control, to feel loved and wanted. However, after going through certain battles in my life, I became addicted to sweets; my husband refers to me as a "sugarholic."

For many years, I used food as a crutch and as a wall to shield myself from my pain. I fuelled my feelings with junk food. I was scared to lose this weight, because if I did I would not have my "crutch" to hold onto. I could not control my impulses to eat. Whether I was hungry or not, I had to eat.

Many of us use food as a crutch—crutches for being unloved, crutches for being taken advantage of, crutches for being dumped... Why do we do this to our bodies? Consciously, we know what we are doing, yet we continue to overeat. We know by eating unhealthily that we are destroying God's temple. Many of us know that we can end up with all sorts of diseases related to unhealthy eating and obesity, yet it is as if we are programmed to eat, so we just continue eating.

Being overweight and not being understood by your spouse can pose problems. It is as though one fuels the other, a cycle that cannot be broken. You feel as if no matter how hard you try, what's the use? He's going to knock you down for trying anyway. If you lose a few pounds and you begin to feel good about yourself, he still manages to negate your efforts, so what do you do? You start eating again, and you try to comfort yourself with food. I tell you, it is a vicious cycle.

How can we break this cycle? Speaking from experience, it is very difficult. Unless the Lord is on your side, helping you, it will be a challenge. Speaking from experience, I thought that the Lord was not hearing my prayers. I did well for a while, but then I returned to my old habits, and the weight just kept coming on. I think it is fear, a fear of the unknown.

I have been overweight for over ten years, and deep down I think that I am afraid to look good or feel good about myself. I am afraid that if I do look and feel the way I did in high school, or even close to it, I may be tempted to revert to my old lifestyle. I have grown so accustomed to my condition that I do not know what I would do if someone said, "Hey, you look good!" It may sound silly to some of you, but there are those of you who may feel the same way.

Nevertheless, there is a way out, ladies. The way out is to take our weight problems to the Lord in prayer. I know the Lord has told me that I will lose my weight; however, it takes two, me and the Lord, so I will have to make a conscious effort to change my eating habits and exercise. Only then will my weight loss take place, and only then will it be permanent.

4

Drug and
Alcohol Abuse

What really leads a person to try drugs and alcohol? Some people do not even know that they are hooked on them. Some people have a drink of wine with their meals on a daily basis. Some people may have a beer from time to time. Others may have hard liquor like rum or vodka on a daily basis just to calm their nerves or to allow themselves to survive.

I stopped drinking over twenty years ago, so I know what I'm talking about. However, I decided before I started having my children that I would not drink anymore, no matter what.

Some of the reasons I drank were due to boredom, frustration, trying to fit in with the crowd, and revenge. Revenge, you may ask? Yes, revenge. In those days, I really was not living for the Lord. Whenever anything or anyone bothered me, I would harbour anger inside, then go out and drink with friends.

Many teenagers, young adults, and adults drink in excess today. After several drinks, many end up being disorderly, embarrassed, and ashamed. Many meet in accidents and some end up dead. Now, is it worth it? Based on the many commercials advertising alcoholic beverages, it is evident that drinking is acceptable in our society.

By the various advertisements that are seen and heard concerning alcohol, the media encourages today's youth to drink. I know that some of my students started drinking in eighth grade; their parents were providing them the alcohol and these students also paid those of legal drinking age to purchase it for them. This is not something new. Unfortunately, a little sip of this and a little sip of that could lead to an addiction.

Alcohol is so powerful and deceptive that it controls lives. I know of a well-educated individual who is an alcoholic and he does not even know it. It is so sad. His wife is always embarrassed for him, his children do not want to be around him. His life is slipping by without him even noticing what the alcohol is doing to him.

Alcohol will bring even the noblest character to shame. I know of a fairly young man who died as a result of liver complications, due to alcohol. When he died, his house was left filthy and littered with empty liquor bottles.

You see, when one becomes an alcoholic, nothing else matters. Once you start drinking casually, it can lead to alcoholism without you knowing it. Drinking can easily become an addiction. If you are in this predicament today, now is the time to pray about it, ask the Lord to help you to overcome it, and seek professional guidance if you cannot do it on your own.

THE SILENT DEATH

DRUG ABUSE

I personally have never taken drugs, so I do not know what it feels like, but I know of friends and students who were into heavy drugs. As a young girl, I saw many teenagers smoking weed. They used to be high most of the time. Over the years, I have seen how their choices affected their education, their chances in life, their jobs, and their relationships.

I had one neighbour in particular who was very handsome, intelligent, and had the potential to be successful in life. However, when he started smoking, he started hanging out with the wrong crowds. He started getting into trouble with the police and his life just took a downward spiral, until the day he married a woman whose influence led him to Christ. He now owns a thriving business and his life has turned around for the better.

I have watched students lose control of their lives due to drug abuse. They dropped out of school, they hung around with the wrong crowd, and many of them ended up in prison. Many of us tried to talk to the young people of today. The teachers and preachers have tried, and parents have tried, but to no avail.

How can we help these young people? Prayer alone is not sufficient. We need to reach out to them with our love and our assistance. If we turn our backs on these youth, how can we face our Maker, and how can we face each other, knowing that we have not done anything to help them? They cannot help themselves. Some of them do not know if they are coming in or going out. Some of them do not know where their next meal is coming from. Just look at the streets of downtown Toronto... it is not difficult to see what I'm talking about. We must find a way to reach these kids before it is too late.

One day when I was on my way to one of my physical therapy sessions, I noticed a young man lying down on the street. He was sleeping, covered with a sleeping bag, and he had an empty cup at his side. As I observed, I realized that people, all kinds of people from every walk of life, passed by him. Some watched him as he slept while others walked by pretending that they did not see him. Deep down, I felt sorry for this young man.

Usually I will give to people who beg on the streets. As long as I have money, I try to give. As I approached the man lying on the street, I took out my coin and I dropped it in his cup. Just as I dropped my coin in his cup, tears started streaming down my face, and I did not know why. I felt so much compassion for the man, yet I did not know what to do to help him. Still crying as I walked away, I heard a voice say to me, *This is the Lord lying there, yet no one knows it and no one cares. They leave him on the street, they stare at him as if he is the worst, the bottom of the barrel, yet they do not know it is Jesus.*

We do not know who we are seeing on the streets. When we see people on drugs, lying in the gutters, it is someone's child. Most importantly, he or she is a child of God. I tell you, I could not stop crying, I felt so sorry that people just left him there and that no one cared to look at him or to help him. I am grateful that I stopped to give him some money, otherwise I would have missed my personal encounter with the Lord. I probably would not have heard that still small voice reminding me of the times that we fail to see Christ in others.

According to the Book of Matthew, Jesus said: *"For I was an hungred, and ye gave me no meat: I was thirsty, and ye gave me no drink: I was a stranger, and ye took me not in: naked, and ye clothed me not: sick, and in prison, and ye visited me not... Inasmuch as ye did it not to one of the least of these, ye did it not to me"* (Matthew 25:42-43,45).

We do not know who we may be passing on the streets, so we must always help others in whatever way we can. The alcoholics and the drug addicts out there are no less than us. Some of them are highly qualified and educated people, some are just lost and do not know where to turn, and some have struggled all their lives. We do not know their situations. We should not focus on who they are now, but who they can become, by the hands of God. It is difficult for some to seek help, but we must pray for them and tell them about Jesus and His love for them. We must ask God to direct us in finding ways to help them. Being an alcoholic or a drug addict is not of God. This is satan's work, and we must defeat satan at all costs.

5
The True Meaning of the Silent Death

What is the true meaning of the silent death? Years ago, when I told my students that I was writing a book entitled *The Silent Death*, they asked me what it was about and what the title meant. At the time, I mentioned to them that it was the many ways that one could die without knowing they were dying. That was the best explanation I had, but as the years went by I realized that it was more than that. The Lord was showing me that I was slowly dying without knowing I was dying as a result of generational curses.

Many Christians believe that because they have accepted Christ as Lord and Saviour, curses cannot affect them. I am here to say that even Christians, born-again, spirit-filled Christians, can be hampered by curses.

What is it and what causes it to affect us? The Concise Oxford Dictionary tells us that "curse" means *"1. A solemn utterance intended to invoke a supernatural power to inflict destruction or punishment on a person or thing. 2. A thing that causes evil or harm."*[1]

Many of us are cursed because of what our ancestors did many years ago. This is called a generational curse. Many of our ancestors were not born-again Christians, and because of this they did things based on their religious beliefs. Sometimes it meant that animals were sacrificed, and because of that, the effects of the evil done at that time were passed down from generation to generation. In some families, the women cannot get married. In other families, the men are worthless drunkards, and they just go around impregnating women all over the place. This is a spirit that is within them, which is a result of generational curses.

I speak as a living example of such curses. I too have struggled with issues and sicknesses throughout my life. One night, I attended a crusade with the hopes of being healed, and when the pastor prayed for me he told me that there was a generational network going on in my life, and that it had to do with my ancestors being Hindu.

I received my deliverance that night, but I must say I was somewhat confused because as long as I had lived, I always believed that my ancestors were Catholics, so I thought to myself, what is he talking about? Low and behold, I was able to talk to an aunt of mine and two older relatives, one of whom was a Pentecostal minister. My cousin told me that my ancestors were Hindus, involved in ritualistic prayers and sacrifices. Bingo! A light bulb went on in my mind.

---

[1] *The Concise Oxford Dictionary (8th Edition)*. Oxford University Press, New York, 1990. p.285

At the crusade, the minister mentioned to me that my illnesses and struggles were a result of what my ancestors had done. Now that I knew the root of the problem, I, through the grace of God, could fix it.

Now I know the true meaning of the silent death. For me, the silent death was a death I was slowly but surely going through. It was a death in every area of my life, caused by ancestral curses. Without me knowing about it, I would have gone through life being sick, rejected, living the valley life, and finally I would have died just thinking it was my time to die, when in fact it would have been a premature death caused by the rituals of my ancestors.

Friends, I am pleading with you to check yourselves. Whether you are a born-again Christian or not, now is the time to pray and ask the Holy Spirit to reveal things to you about your ancestors. If it means you have to pray about what they did in the past so that the Lord can reveal what you have to do now in order to escape from their curses, now is the time to heed that call. Now is the time to really pray and pray like you have never prayed before. Ask God to deliver you from all ancestral curses.

I thank God for setting me free and for revealing to me what was killing me both spiritually and physically. You know you are dying when every area of your life is being affected: your health, your spiritual life, your career, your finances, and your marriage. Your destiny is being tampered with, and these are just some of the signs I experienced.

Some of you may notice that even your relationships are in trouble. How many of you help others and the same people you help turn around and stab you in the back for no reason? I used to think that it was only women who did that to me. That's what it seemed like. I have helped so many women and the majority of them turned their backs on me. Some even cursed me and stopped speaking to me, despite the times when I had been there for them.

It used to bother me, even to the point that I gave up on having close women friends. I put up a wall around me, and I only allowed my sister Claudette in. If I noticed that any woman wanted to be my close friend, I would put up a barrier for fear of being hurt again.

You may think I was being selfish, but at the time I did not think so. It was a matter of survival. I had been hurt so badly in the past by women that I would always keep their friendship at arm's length. All this time, I did not realize that it was the demonic networking that had my life the way it was. Praise God for His revelation power and for His deliverance. You too can have God's revelation and deliverance. Just ask Him. He will do it for you.

6
The Way Out of Bondage

What is the way out of bondage? The Bible tells us in Psalm 37:1-3: *"Fret not thyself because of evildoers, neither be thou envious against the workers of iniquity. For they shall soon be cut down like the grass, and wither as the green herb. Trust in the Lord, and do good; so shalt thou dwell in the land, and verily thou shalt be fed."*

The Lord is telling us that we should not worry about those who do us evil; we should not fret ourselves, because He will deal with them. In God's time, he will bring them to naught. The Lord also stated that we should not be envious against the workers of iniquity. Do not be jealous if you see the unsaved acquiring all the wealth—you do not know where it is coming from. Some may be thieves, and some may be doing injustices to acquire the wealth, so do not be envious or jealous of them.

I remember seeing on the news recently. A CEO of a large company was being charged for defrauding his company and the public. This man made millions of dollars by wrongdoings. Now tell me, why should I be jealous of him? The Bible says to trust in the Lord, to do good, and the Lord is going to provide for us. We do not have to be jealous of anyone.

I know some of us get jealous of our co-workers when they get the big promotion instead of us, but let us look at it this way: the Lord is the one who promotes us, so when it is God's time for us to be promoted, we will be promoted. Many of us try to rush God. We try to tell God when to do things and even how to do things, but that is not how we should live. We should be in tune with God at all times, we should be depending on Him, and we should be waiting on Him to direct our lives, to lead us where He wants us to be, instead of the other way around.

Tell me, what does it profit a man to lose his own soul? By this, I am saying that when we go after the things that are not of God, just to be with the in-crowd, or to look good in front of our peers, what good is that doing for us? At the end of the day, doing the wrong things, being in the wrong places, and fighting against each other will not make us happier people.

Twenty-three years ago, we moved from an apartment to our first house. Kristin, my daughter, was only nine months old. The apartment we were living in was an adult only apartment, so Andy decided we should buy a house. The house we bought was a semi-detached bungalow. I was so happy, but it only took a few months for me to realize that I did not care for the house. I wanted to move.

I had always wanted a house with a double garage, a fireplace, four bedrooms, and a patio. For fourteen years, I waited to get my dream home. Finally, the day arrived. I moved into the home that

I had always wanted. I have been living here for nine years now, and I must say, it means nothing. I thought I would have been happy having all this, but the happiness was not long-lasting. You see, I am saying all this to say that sometimes we go after material things that give us instant gratification and instant happiness, but what we should be going after are the things that will give us everlasting gratification.

The way out of our bondage is Salvation. I cannot stress enough that accepting Jesus as your Lord and Saviour is of vital importance! This is the first step in the way to everlasting freedom, everlasting happiness, and life everlasting. The Bible tells us in John 3:16, *"For God so loved the world, that he gave his only begotten Son, that whosoever believeth in him should not perish, but have everlasting life."*

The second step to our way out is through Obedience. We must obey God. The Bible tells us in Acts 5:29 that we must obey God rather than men. This simply means that, no matter what situation we are in, we should obey God's words over those of others. Sometimes we may want something so badly that we swear that the voice we heard regarding certain things was that of God, but we know deep down that it is our own voice we are hearing. So do not fool yourself. Fooling yourself will only put you in deeper trouble and frustration. Trust God, obey Him, and His will for your life will be fulfilled.

The third step to our way out is Trust. Trust in God. Trust Him where you cannot sense Him. Trust Him in the morning, noon, and night. When you trust God, when you wait on Him, He will deliver you. He will provide all your needs. He will promote you, He will set you free, and He will bless you. Some of us put our trust in man, some of us put our trust in the lottery, and some of us put our trust in the palm readers and psychics. Nevertheless, I am here to tell you that the palm readers and psychics are workers of the devil. They will lead you to destruction. They will lead you to places where you should not be, and ultimately they will lead you to Hell. Hell is real, believe me.

The fourth step to our way out is Patience. So many of us are impatient. You can see it in the morning commute to work. People are so rushed that sometimes we see them swearing because they cannot get ahead in traffic. We do not realize that when we are in the traffic, that is the time to pray and sing songs to the Lord. It is the perfect time to commune with God. Thank God for the traffic jam, because who knows? Maybe you could have gotten into an accident. So give God praise for the traffic situation. Let us learn to be patient, let us learn not to rush, rush, rush all the time.

The fifth step to our way out is reading God's word, the Bible. This is a very important step in getting out of bondage. God's word is pure, it is holy, and it is His direction for our lives. If we just pray and do not read God's word on a daily basis, it is like going on a boat without a life jacket. The Lord's word is sharper than a two-edged sword. It cuts deep within us, it teaches us, it comforts us, it helps us, and it directs our lives. When I need to hear from God, I simply ask the Holy Spirit to lead me to the scripture I should be reading for that specific day and that specific hour. I tell you, the Lord has never failed me. He has always directed me!

The sixth step to our way out is Love. The Bible tells us in Galatians 5:22, *"But the fruit of the Spirit is love, joy, peace, longsuffering, gentleness, goodness, faith."* We must love God, love our neighbour, love ourselves, and most of all love our enemies. I can hear you saying to me, "Love our enemies?!" Yes, love our enemies. We must forgive them and love them. I am not saying that you should go out of your way to be around them. I am saying, you must love them. It is by you loving them that our Father in Heaven will forgive you and love you even more.

The seventh step to our way out is Forgiveness. We must, must, must forgive. This is a difficult one, I know. I had to really search myself and ask God to help me with this one. As I mentioned before, so many people have hurt me over the years. The worst situation is when your closest friends and family do you wrong. I tell you, it took time, but God took away the hurt and the pain from me, and I was able to forgive them. To be honest, since I let them go, since I forgave them, a peace has come over me. It has been like I was no longer trapped by the pain they had caused me. I was set free.

Sisters and brothers who may be reading this book, there is definitely a way out of our oppression and bondage. I guarantee that if you open up your heart, let Jesus in, live for Him, trust Him, be patient, learn to love, and forgive, you will be set free. You will be happy. You will have a joy in your heart and a purpose to your life. Just trust Him, have faith in Him, and let God be God in your lives. Only then, you will have the victory.

7
Who Are We?

Have you ever wondered who we are and why we are here? I know I have. Sometimes I wonder why I was brought into this world to experience all the hardships, the torment, the failure, the hurt, the pain, and the frustrations of life. I thought that that was God's way of getting my attention and His way of teaching me to trust in Him and to depend on Him.

I was at a crusade one night and the preacher's topic was entitled, "Living Above Illegal Interference." I was amazed at what I learned that night. The pastor said that God had a plan for our lives since before we were born. Just think, when a building has to be built, you need the architects to put plans in place. It is the same with God. Before we were born, our God already had a plan for our lives, who we would be, what we would do, and who we would become.

The Lord was talking to Jeremiah when He stated, *"Before I formed thee in the belly I knew thee; and before thou camest forth out of the womb I sanctified thee, and I ordained thee a prophet unto the nations"* (Jeremiah 1:5). The Lord is saying here that even before we are born, the blueprint for our lives was already in place.

The pastor at the crusade went on to say that before we were born, there is a book in which our names are written. In that book, everything that God has for our lives is recorded: our blessings, our life story, and all that we have to accomplish here on earth. In other words, God knows us. We cannot hide from Him. He knows what we are going to do for Him. He knows the lies we tell even before we tell them. God sees everything and knows it all. All that we are to accomplish is written in our book.

The pastor also mentioned that failure, hurt, poverty, sickness, disease, and trials are not written in our book. These are things that are imposed on us by satan. These things happen throughout our lives because we permit them to happen. Do not misunderstand what I am trying to say: obviously, we do not consciously let sickness come upon us, nor allow poverty to strike us. The pastor was saying that through our lack of knowledge, and our lack of obedience to God, the enemy has done these things to us. Therefore, in our book that the Lord has of our lives, all the negative things in our lives are not recorded, which means they should not have been there in the first place. They should never have happened to us.

The Bible tells us that, *"The Kingdom of heaven is likened unto a man which sowed good seed in his field: but while men slept, his enemy came and sowed tares among the wheat, and went his way"* (Matthew 13:24-25). The Lord is saying here that, while we slept, the enemy came in. Sleeping here does not only mean physically sleeping, with our eyes closed. It means that when we became Christians, we were on fire for the Lord. After a while, blessings started coming our way, so we got comfortable. Then, when we noticed the blessings, we got lazy, and that is when we hardly read God's words. We could not find the time to pray anymore, because of the wife, the husband, the kids, the soccer lessons, the dance classes, or the music classes. You know what I'm talking about—we fell asleep.

The times when we used to meet with God, the intimate moments, the time when we could not wait to whisper to Him, quickly vanished. Some of us do not even have time to have our family devotion anymore; it used to be nightly, but now it is just once in a while. This is when the enemy comes in. It is when we are sleeping that the enemy comes in.

No one can write sickness, poverty, death, or anything else in God's book unless we permit it. By not praying, by not reading God's words, by not communing with God on a regular, whole-hearted basis, the enemy writes these negative things in each of our books. You may say that it is mean for me to say these things, but I am also speaking about myself. Here is a reminder: I have been on sick leave for four years now. I too allowed my enemy to write sickness in my book, poverty in my book, disappointment and frustration in my book. How did I do it? At some point in my life, I was too busy for God, busy with everything else, and when it came to praying and spending time in God's Words, I too slept.

I am not saying that this is the end of me or that this is the end for you. For even the date, time, and place of our deaths are recorded in our book. This tells me that God is not only the Author, but also the Finisher of our lives. Unless the Lord is ready for us to meet Him, no matter what the enemy throws at us, we will not die. The Bible states, *"For I know the thoughts that I think toward you, saith the Lord, thoughts of peace, and not of evil, to give you an expected end"* (Jeremiah 29:11).

This is just to show you that all the struggles, all the hardship, and all the setbacks we are going through are just a stage in our lives. This is not the end of our lives. The enemy came in like a thief in the night, to rob, to steal, and to destroy us, but God did not write in our books that we must suffer, or that we must be living from paycheque to paycheque. We must not suffer that silent death, or any death for that matter, unless God calls us home to be with Him. The Lord Jesus Christ wants our lives to be a blessing.

I know what it is like not to have a paycheque. For the past four years, I have been denied disability for my illness, although I have a doctor's report stating that I cannot perform my duties as a teacher. Andy, my husband, has been laid off from his work for over three years. Thank God he received a package which enables us to pay the mortgage, the bills, our daughter Kristin's university fees, and we are able to put aside for our son Gregory's college fees.

Recently, Kristin told me that I needed some new clothes, because she was tired of seeing me in my old clothes. I thought that I had hit rock bottom with regards to my financial situation. Sometimes I felt ashamed to go to church, knowing that I did not have a dollar to put in the offering plate. I really mean ashamed, because in my church, you had to get out of your seat to go to the front to put the offering in the container. There are days when I do not have anything to give. Sometimes the pastor of the church will ask for a special offering to give to the visiting ministers, and in my heart I want to give, but I do not have the funds. I know what it is like to be in want. Just note that even in my wanting stage, the Lord has always provided for me.

I remember Greg having to go to a college fair with his high school. He is preparing for college next year, and the head of guidance, knowing my situation, offered to pay the six dollars needed for the trip. This is when it hit me, that I had hit the financial rock bottom!

Brethren, it is not easy being robbed of what God has in store for us. Poverty is not of God. Sickness is not of God. Negative living is not of God. It is all from satan. So please, let us pray for forgiveness, direction in our lives, and let us pray to God to change our destiny so that it lines up with what He has written in His book for our lives.

8

The Deep Thoughts of God

Have you ever wondered what God's thoughts are about you? Sometimes I ask myself, "What is God thinking about when it comes to me?" I must tell you, sometimes I am ashamed when I think about all the promises I have made to God and did not keep. This book, for example, should have been written and published many years ago, yet I am still writing it. How God must be disappointed in me.

God must be thinking that I am slow, I am lackadaisical, and that I procrastinate too much. I know I have been a procrastinator ever since high school. I used to consistently delay completing my assignments until the last minute, and then I would hustle to complete them, sometimes barely earning a passing grade as a result. If I had taken the time to plan, write, edit, and then rewrite my assignments, on many occasions I would have achieved higher marks.

At times, I think that God does not hear my prayers. I question God as to why my prayers are not being answered and why I am in some situations which seem to go on forever. Sometimes I think that financially, I am at the bottom of the barrel and that if I was to get any lower, I would have to beg on the streets. That is just the way I feel sometimes. Why God, why?

Why do we have to work so hard and struggle so hard? As Christians, things should come easy for us. We see the non-Christians out there reaping all the benefits, and getting the great paying jobs, and it is as though they are living on top of the world. And to think, they don't know the Lord as their personal Saviour. So why should we as children of God suffer? We are known as princes and princesses, because we are children of the King, so why, Lord? Why do we feel as if we are forgotten?

To know the thoughts of God, we have to pray and read God's words. The Lord is telling us that we should not look at the outward things, but that we should look inwardly. We must not look at our circumstances. We must look up from whence cometh our help. The Lord God Almighty is telling us that we are continually in His thoughts.

I know of an adage that states, "God's eyes may be closed, but he is not sleeping. He is just resting." Even when God's eyes are resting, He still sees us. *He knows* our pain, *He knows* our weaknesses, *He knows* what we are going through, and in *His time*, we will get our answers.

I remember a sermon I heard a pastor preaching once. It was about Daniel. When Daniel prayed, he did not get an answer from God. In Daniel 10:12-13, the Bible tells us that when Daniel prayed, God answered right away, but it was satan who intercepted God's answers from reaching him. Michael, one of the chief princes, went to help fight satan in order for the answers to reach Daniel. This is proof that God always answers our prayers, but it is satan who prevents the answers from reaching us.

To ensure that there is no confusion, please note that God cares for us all, He knows our weaknesses and our strengths, and He knows that we have good intentions to pray and read His words. He also knows when we fall asleep while reading His words. He has us in His thoughts morning, noon, and night. God is constantly reaching out to us in different ways. Sometimes we hear Him and sometimes we ignore Him.

God's thoughts toward us are of peace, love, joy, happiness, accomplishment, success, salvation, deliverance, and most of all for us to fulfill His plans for our lives. The Lord God Almighty did not bring us into this world to leave us here on our own. He did not allow us to be born without there being a plan and purpose for us to fulfill. In other words, we must seek God to know His intentions for us. We must know what God's thoughts are concerning us, so that we can accomplish God's will for our lives.

I personally would have considered myself a failure if I had not completed this book for the Lord, because I know this is God's will for my life. I have to accomplish this task. You must first ask God what His will is concerning your life, and then at all costs you must accomplish it.

If you cannot accomplish it, at least give it your all, so that when you meet God, you can tell him, "I made the effort." Will that be good enough? What do you think?

9
Swallowed Blessings

As I have mentioned time and time again that our Father in Heaven bestows upon us daily blessings, blessings that we sometimes cannot imagine. Sometimes when I look back on my life and see where God has brought me from, that alone is a mighty blessing!

Our Father loves us. He cares for us. Let me reiterate this fact: Our God does not want to see us suffer. He does not want to see us beg. Many of us today are begging. Although we may not be on the streets begging, we are still begging. If the Lord Jesus Christ could open our spiritual eyes, we would realize that we should not beg for anything, because our Father in Heaven has it all for us. All He has is ours; God wants us to be rich, in every sense of the word. He wants us to be rich in every area of our lives: in our academics, in our careers, in our marriages, in our finances, in our homes, in our relationship with our children, and in our workplace. God wants us to prosper and He wants us to succeed in every area of our lives.

For all of us, when we pray, God answers us right away, but as I mentioned before, those answers sometimes do not come to us because of the demons that swallow our blessings. Let me explain. When we pray, the angels of the Living God take our requests to the Father, God answers us immediately—sometimes it is the answer we are hoping for, and sometimes it is not the answer we are hoping for. When it is not the answer we are looking for, we should not be dismayed.

Here is an example: a few years ago, my son Gregory asked me to buy him a Rossini bike. I said no, because my cousin died in his twenties while riding a motorbike. Knowing teenagers, when I said no, he then went to his dad and asked the same question. My husband said yes. Lo and behold, within a few days the Rossini bike was in my driveway.

Greg knew how I felt about it, but I told him I would bless it anyway. Honestly, I prayed over that bike. I anointed it and I asked God to always protect him when he was on it. I said an honest prayer. You must believe me, although Greg thinks otherwise. Greg was able to ride it only in the neighbourhood, but within a few weeks the bike stopped working. Of course, Greg blamed me and even said that I had put a curse on the bike for it not to work. It sat in the garage for weeks, until finally he found out what was wrong and he ordered the part and fixed it. Within one or two days, however, it broke down again. Right now, it is still sitting in the garage.

You see, sometimes God will answer you, but if He knows that something is bad for you or that it might kill you, He will do one of two things: He will give it to you for a while, just like He did for Greg, or He will not give it to you at all. You see, Greg wanted this bike so badly that God enabled him to have it, but God knows that maybe if he were to ride it often, he could get into an accident or something, so the Lord has allowed it not to work.

The Lord always knows when to bless us, how to bless us, and how much to bless us with. You see, there are daily blessings for us to have. Yes, daily. Our Father in Heaven blesses us daily. The Bible states that *"He shall receive the blessing from the Lord, and righteousness from the God of his salvation"* (Psalm 24:5). The Bible also tells us that *"the thief cometh not, but for to steal, and to kill, and to destroy: I am come that they might have life, and that they might have it more abundantly"* (John 10:10). Therefore, when God bestows His blessings on us, satan, that old devil, is right there to swallow our blessings.

satan has his demons, his agents, and his angels out there just waiting for God to dispense His blessings on us. As soon as God gives His angels the blessings to bring to us, satan's angels prevent them from reaching us. That is why our blessings, yours and mine, are not reaching us. So for those of you who are praying and praying and praying for that one thing for years, whether it is salvation for your loved ones, whether it is for your deliverance, whether it is your finances, whether it is for your career, just note one thing: God already blessed us, but satan and his agents have prevented them from reaching us.

What is the way out? How do we get those blessings back from satan? We rage war against him. We fight with fasting and praying and we command that every blessing that has been stolen from us be returned by the Blood of Jesus Christ, in the name of Jesus. This is not easy. Sometimes you have to fight with all you have in order to obtain your blessings.

I remember when I just got saved, over twenty years ago, my first pastor preached a sermon one Sunday. He said, "So many Christians are blessed with tremendous blessings, yet these blessings are never brought to fruition." He continued to say, "As Christians, we give up too easily and sometimes the answer, and our blessings, are right around the corner. All we have to do is tie a knot and hang on." He said, "Tie that knot and hang on because your answer is right around the corner. If you let go or give up, you will never get your answer, you will never get your blessing!"

How many of us tie that knot? How many of us, including myself, really tie that knot and hang on when we have been praying for months, sometimes even years? Many of us missed our blessings because we did not have the faith to hang on. Brethren, please listen to me. Our loving Father sits on His throne. He is there to bless us, to provide for us. He blesses us daily, He answers our prayers, but satan robs us of our blessings. satan even gives these blessings to other people. For example, you have been praying for a promotion for years, and when your name is finally called for a promotion, something happens and the promotion goes to someone else. Some ministers have referred to this as "transference of blessings."

Do not allow satan to rob you anymore of your blessings. Do not let his demons swallow what God has for you. Check yourselves. Are you truly living for God? Are you fasting and praying? Are you obeying God? If you have said yes to these questions and you are not getting your blessings, then satan is robbing you of them. If you are not living for Jesus, now would be a good time to accept Him and live for Him.

Although we may think we are living a good, clean Christian life, let us check ourselves again. Do we envy the success of our church brothers and sisters? Are we spending time gossiping about others?

We need to check ourselves daily, because these are the things satan uses against us when God is ready to bless us. Brothers and sisters, it is time that we stand up and fight for what we believe in. We must take back everything that satan has robbed from us. It is time for our children to return to Christ. It is time for our lives to glorify God. We should be free from sin in order for us to receive God's blessings. When we sin, ask God's forgiveness. We must make our way clear so that when God is ready to bless us, the blessings will flow.

From this day forward, pray and ask God to open the Heavens for you. An open Heaven means that God will pour out His riches, His glory, and all His blessings upon you. No matter what, God's angels will fight for you so that you will receive what God has for your life. However, you and I must do our part also—we must live a holy life, we must check ourselves daily, we must humble ourselves, and we must fight the good fight—in order to have our stolen blessings returned to us.

10

The Revelation Power of God

Revelation is the last book in the New Testament. According to the Concise Oxford Dictionary, "revelation" means, "*an act or an instance of revealing, especially the supposed disclosure of knowledge to humankind by a divine or supernatural agency.*"[2] In the Bible, the book of Revelation informs us of things to come.

The Bible tells us that, "*Behold, he cometh with clouds; and every eye shall see him, and they also which pierced him: and all kindreds of the earth shall wail because of him. Even so, Amen*" (Revelation 1:7). The Lord Jesus Christ is speaking in verse eight. He says, "*I am Alpha and Omega, the beginning and the ending, saith*

---

[2] *The Concise Oxford Dictionary (8th Edition)*. Oxford University Press, New York, 1990. p.1031

the Lord, which is, and which was, and which is to come, the Almighty" (Revelation 1:8).

Many people do not believe that Jesus Christ is coming back again. Many people do not believe that Jesus died, rose from the dead, and will be coming back for us. I have spoken to so many people who have told me that Jesus was only a prophet, and that Jesus died, but that He is not coming back again. However, the Bible tells us that Jesus Christ will come again and that every eye shall see Him.

As a child growing up in the West Indies, the Christian children in my school would often say that Jesus Christ is coming back for us and we have to be ready. I did not have a clue as to what they were talking about. My only concept of Jesus was the statue of Him in the Catholic church.

In my high school, I heard other people talking about Jesus coming back again. At the time, I was not born again, so I did not have any understanding of what they were talking about. It was only when I accepted Jesus Christ as my Lord and Saviour that I gained the knowledge that Jesus died for me, and that He is coming back again for us. This is evident in Revelation 22. Jesus declared that He is coming back for us. Please do not take this statement lightly.

What is the revelation power of God? The Lord said that He knows our works, our charity, our service, and our faith (Revelation 2:19). He went on to say in Revelation, *"I know thy works, that thou art neither cold nor hot: I would thou wert cold or hot. So then because thou art lukewarm, and neither cold nor hot, I will spew thee out of my mouth"* (Revelation 3:15-16).

Later in the same chapter, Jesus said, *"Behold, I stand at the door, and knock: if any man hear my voice, and open the door, I will come in to him, and will sup with him, and be with me.* To him that *overcometh will I grant to sit with me in my throne, even as I also overcame, and am set down with my Father in his throne"* (Revelation 3:20-21).

The Lord Jesus Christ is inviting us to accept Him as our Lord and Saviour, to live for Him, so that in the end He will be able to take us to His Father. If we do not accept Jesus as our Lord and Saviour, we will not make it into Heaven. We will go to Hell.

In Revelation 12, the Bible tells us that satan and his angels were cast out of Heaven and that he is on earth to deceive the whole world. satan knows that he is here only for a short time so he uses all he knows to deceive us, to steal from us, and to destroy us. Nevertheless, please note that through Jesus' death, His shed Blood, and His resurrection, we will *always* have victory over satan.

Once you accept Jesus as your Lord and Saviour, your name is written down in the Book of Life. The Bible tells us in John 3 that there was a man of the Pharisees named Nicodemus, a ruler of the Jews. Nicodemus went to Jesus and told Him that he knew that Jesus was a teacher who came from God because no man could perform the miracles that Jesus did except if God was with him. (John 3:1-2)

Jesus answered and said unto Nicodemus, *"Verily, verily I say unto thee, Except a man be born again, he cannot see the kingdom of God"* (John 3:3). Jesus continued and said to Nicodemus, *"That whosoever believeth in Him should not perish, but have eternal life. For God so loved the world, that he gave his only begotten Son, that whosoever believeth in Him should not perish, but have everlasting life. For God sent not his Son into the world to condemn the world;*

but that the world through Him might be saved. He that believeth on Him is not condemned: but he that believeth not is condemned already, because he hath not believed in the name of the only begotten Son of God" (John 3:15-18). Jesus is telling Nicodemus that we must be born again, which means we must accept Jesus Christ as our Lord and Saviour, and it is by doing so that we will make it into Heaven and have everlasting life.

The Bible says, in Revelation 13:1-18, that *"a beast [rises] out of the sea, having seven heads and ten horns, and upon his horns ten crowns, and upon his heads the name of blasphemy. And the beast which I saw was like unto a leopard, and his feet were as the feet of a bear, and his mouth as the mouth of a lion: and the dragon gave him his power, and his seat, and great authority."*

In verses three onward, the Bible continues to say that people worshipped the dragon which gave power unto the beast, and they worshipped the beast. The beast was given a mouth *"and he opened his mouth in blasphemy against God, to blaspheme his name, and his tabernacle, and them that dwell in Heaven... All that dwell upon the earth shall worship him, whose names are not written in the book of life of the Lamb slain from the foundation of the world"* (Revelation 13:6,8).

The beast will deceive all that dwell on the earth by the means of miracles. He will also cause *"both small and great, rich and poor, free and bond, to receive a mark in their right hand, or in their foreheads: and that no man might buy or sell, save he that had the mark, or the name of the beast, or the number of his name... for it is the number... six hundred threescore and six"* (Revelation 13:16-18).

Our God is revealing to us things to come. We must be aware of these things. Many of us have heard about the number 666 and many of us may not know about the number of the beast. Beware, the Bible tells us that those who take the number 666, *"The same shall drink of the wine of the wrath of God, which is poured out without mixture into the cup of his indignation; and he shall be tormented with fire and brimstone in the presence of the holy angels, and in the presence of the Lamb"* (Revelation 14:10)

Those who follow the beast and take his number will have eternal life with the beast in Hell. Those who do not worship the beast, neither his image nor take his mark upon their foreheads or in their hands, they will live and reign with Christ a thousand years.

Those who stand firm, stand fast, and wait on the Lord, those who live for Jesus Christ, no matter the suffering they have to endure here on Earth while the beast is presiding, they are the ones who will make it into Heaven.

Brothers and sisters, saved and unsaved, please listen to me: Heaven is real and Hell is also real. The choice is yours to make. Only you can make that choice. I cannot make it for you. Your husband or wife cannot make that choice for you. The point is that you have to decide right now where you want to spend eternity. You cannot say you haven't heard of what will happen in the coming days, because the Lord has warned us. The mark of the beast is real, it is coming, and so is Jesus Christ. He is coming back for His people, the ones who love Him, accept Him, live for Him, obey Him, and the ones who endure. Please be one of them who will say yes to Jesus.

Sometimes I feel very sad when I see prostitutes on the streets who do not know what to do to make it in life. Many of these young women are forced into this lifestyle. They work the streets just to make ends meet. Others do it because they believe they are worthless and that no one cares for them. I hope at least one prostitute will get a chance to read this book and turn her life around. I want her to know that what she is doing is wrong. She is defiling the temple of God, and by doing what she is doing, she is making her way straight to Hell.

If you are not living for Jesus, it means that you are living for the devil. satan, that devil, will use your mind against you. He will tell you that you are not good enough to amount to anything, and that you are worth the money you are making in this trade. However, I am here to tell you that as a prostitute you are robbing yourself. You are not only robbing yourself, but you are also robbing God. God created you in His own image and God desires to live in you. Your body is His temple, so if you abuse your body, and if you let every Tom, Dick, Harry, or Jane abuse it, you are offending God.

The Lord Jesus Christ cannot live in you when you are selling His temple to everyone. Our God is a jealous God. He has equipped you with many talents and gifts in order for you to make a decent, respectable living, so *please*, if you think that this is the only job you can do, think again. Think of the talents you have, the knowledge you have, and the resources out there that can help you get off the streets and into the place where you really belong. No one belongs on the streets as a prostitute. Just think, who is making the money off of you? It is the pimps and the scum that satan uses to carry out his destruction.

Ladies, young women, teenagers, you are all wonderfully and beautifully made in God's image. Do not believe that this is all you can do, because it is not, there are better jobs out there for you, if you would just accept Jesus. Seek help and trust God; He will enable you to do better and to live the life He wants you to live.

I know of a woman who is married and has children. Her husband and children are not aware that she is a prostitute. I will refer to her as Kathy (this is not her real name). As Kathy goes about her daily activities, one would never guess that she lives a dual life. She appears to be the epitome of a wife and mother. She is always well dressed, very articulate, and she appears to have it all together. We have had the opportunity to exchange small talk on several occasions. However, it took a while for me to find out that she was a prostitute. She always talked about how busy she was at work and how tired she was each day as she returned home to cook and clean. When I found out about her lifestyle, I was shocked, but I never looked upon her with disdain. Instead, I was merely concerned about the choice that she had made. At that point, it occurred to me that satan is really out there to rob, steal, and destroy.

satan keeps telling this woman that she is nothing unless she sells herself. Kathy tries to give the world the impression that she has it all, but deep down, Kathy is empty, lonely, frustrated, and in need of salvation and deliverance.

Unfortunately, Kathy's lifestyle stems from relatives who have engaged in prostitution for generations. Although she is aware that this lifestyle is immoral, it results in quick and easy money. The only thing I can do for her is to pray for her and trust that the Lord will save her and deliver her from this curse.

Please listen to me. I know what it feels like to be lonely, frustrated, and depressed. I know what it feels like not to have a penny to your name... but to become a prostitute is not the solution. I am sure there are other ways to make a living. It is not easy, I know. Sometimes you will have to want to do better badly enough for things to turn around in your life.

So many prostitutes in our society want to change. They really want to get off the streets and do better for themselves. However, their attempts to break free of the cycle are useless unless they are helped. How many of us try to talk to them instead of looking down on them? How many of us pass them as if they are the filth of the earth? How many of us really care about these women?

Let me tell you something. It could be your daughter out there in the streets. satan is not a respecter of persons; he can take my daughter, your daughter, any girl out there from their young age, and sow that seed into them. satan, the old devil, can plant lust in their minds, sexual demons in their bodies, lies in their heads, to turn them and place them on the streets.

The Bible tells us that upon his return, Jesus *"hath judged the great whore, which did corrupt the earth with her fornication"* (Revelation 19:2). This means that unless we do something about this epidemic, our young girls, our daughters, our sisters, and our mothers will be judged by God and they will go to Hell if they do not repent and accept Jesus as their Lord and Saviour.

God has many promises for us, as seen throughout Revelation. I cannot end this chapter without mentioning that the Lord Jesus Christ is coming back again. This is a promise of God. He said that in the last days, there shall be earthquakes, floods, disasters, and sicknesses poured out unto the lands, and truly we can see these things taking place today; we know that we are in the last days.

When Jesus returns, He said that the devil will be bound for a thousand years. The Lord will cast satan into the bottomless pit, and shut him up, and set a seal upon him, that he should deceive the nations no more, till the thousand years should be fulfilled: and after that, he must be loosed a little season (Revelation 20: 2-3)

The Bible states also that there will be a new Heaven and a new Earth and that God will dwell with us and *"wipe away all tears from their eyes; and there shall be no more death, neither sorrow, nor crying, neither shall there be any more pain: for the former things are passed away"* (Revelation 21:4). The Lord said that He will make all things new. He also says, *"I am Alpha and Omega, the beginning and the end. I will give unto him that is athirst of the fountain of the water of life freely"* (Revelation 21:6).

God said to us that *"he that overcometh shall inherit all things... but the fearful, and unbelieving, and the abominable, and murderers, and whoremongers, and sorcerers, and idolaters, and all liars, shall have their part in the lake which burneth with fire and brimstone: which is the second death"* (Revelation 21:7-8).

In Revelation 22, the Lord is stressing His promises. He says, *"Behold, I come quickly; and my reward is with me, to give every man according as his work shall be. I am Alpha and Omega, the beginning and the end, the first and the last"* (Revelation 22:12-13).

Our Lord God Almighty is revealing to us the things to come. Take heed, listen, and do not fool around and have pity parties with your life. God is warning us that He is coming back again, and it will be when we least expect it. It could be when one of us Christians is in a worldly night club, thinking that our pastor and no one else from our church is watching us. It could be when we are having an affair with a fellow Christian. It could be when we are plotting and scheming against our brethren. Or it could be when we are lying down with our regular prostitute.

Young women and men who are reading this book, you are not reading this by accident. God intended for you to read this book. He is telling us all to know Him, love Him, live for Him, and obey Him, because He is recording everything we do here on earth in His book, and one day we will have to account for everything in that book. Soon and very soon, the Lord Jesus Christ is coming back again. Some of us will make it into Heaven with Him, while some of us will go to Hell. Now is your chance to make that decision as to where you want to spend eternity. So which will it be: Heaven or Hell?

11
A Woman's Virtue

WOMEN

Women are important to God. Mary, Jesus' mother, was a virtuous woman. So many women we see in the Bible were virtuous women. What is a virtuous woman? A virtuous woman is a woman who has high morals. She is good, she has excellent qualities, and she lives upright. In Proverbs 31, the Bible states that, "*Who can find a virtuous woman? for her price is far above rubies. The heart of her husband doth safely trust in her, so that he shall have no need of spoil. She will do him good and not evil all the days of her life... She stretcheth out her hand to the poor; yea, she reacheth forth her hands to the needy... She openeth her mouth with wisdom; and in her tongue is the law of kindness. She looketh well to the ways of her household, and eateth not the bread of idleness. Her children arise up, and call her blessed; her husband also, and he praiseth her. Many daughters have done virtuously, but thou excellest them all. Favour is deceitful, and beauty is vain: but a woman that feareth the Lord, she shall be praised"* (Proverbs 31:10-12,20,26-30).

In other words, a virtuous woman must be different from the common woman. Her heart must be pure, she must be selfless, and she must be good at all times, no matter the circumstance. A virtuous woman is a giver and a worker. She is honourable and just. She displays strength and, most importantly, she fears the Lord. This means she obeys God and lives wholeheartedly for God.

The Lord is calling on us to be virtuous women. Do not misunderstand my point. I am not saying that the Lord will not call a non-virtuous woman; I am saying that God wants us to be virtuous women. Our virtue is what makes us good women. The way we live, the way we carry ourselves, makes us virtuous women.

Why do you think God chose Mary to be Jesus' mother? She was pure, she was holy, she was a good woman, she was kind, and she did not have a blemish in any area of her life. That is why God used her to be Jesus' mother. You might say, "Juliet, I can't be like Mary." I am not asking you to be like Mary. I am simply saying that as women, we should strive to be selfless, pure, kind, loving, and fearful of God. Only then can we be considered virtuous women.

DAUGHTERS

Let us start with our morals. What standards do we live by? What morals are we passing on to our daughters? I will tell you that whatever you do as a mother, your daughters will follow. If you are a Christian, your daughters will live the Christian life. I am not going to use the term Christian in any old way. When I say Christian, I am speaking about really living for the Lord. If you are smoking and drinking every day and partying every weekend, that is all your daughters will know and that is all they will continue to do.

If you are a woman who likes to get men's attention wherever you go, if you are the type that has to wear tight fitting clothes, low-cut dresses, mini skirts, and heavy makeup, that is what your daughters will want to do. I am not lying. One day, I was at the drugstore and a lady was teaching people how to put on makeup, so my daughter Kristin encouraged me to give it a try, because God knows I needed a lift in that area. I decided to sit and wait to get my free makeup on. I only agreed to get it done because I was meeting with some high school friends that night, and I really wanted to look special. While I was waiting to get my makeup done, a little girl and her mother were having their makeup done. The child was arguing with her mother, telling her how she wanted her makeup applied. The mother turned to me and said she did not know what to do, because all the girls in her daughter's school were wearing heavy makeup, but she (the mother) was not in favour of it because her daughter was only thirteen.

I turned to the lady and said, "You have got to be kidding, your daughter is only thirteen and is wearing makeup already!" I told the lady that Kristin had only been allowed to wear face powder and lip gloss at that age, and even now at nineteen, she wears very little makeup. I then told her daughter that she was too young, and that she was pretty without it. I reminded the mother that allowing her daughter to wear makeup at this age would only encourage boys to take advantage of her, because she would appear to be an older girl. The mother agreed with me, but was unable to convince her daughter that wearing heavy makeup at that age was inappropriate.

My goal is not to discuss whether wearing makeup is right or wrong. Some Christians wear makeup while others do not. My main purpose is to illustrate that as women, what we do and say will inevitably impact our daughters, sisters, aunts, cousins, and the young women we interact with everyday.

As women, we should aspire to set good examples for younger girls and other women to follow. We must consider how our conduct will affect the next generation. We shouldn't pretend to be who we are not. We must be ourselves, be kind, be gentle, and be straightforward with people. Our standards on our jobs, at home, at church, in our neighbourhood, and in every area of our lives should be high.

Teenagers

As a teenaged girl, you should strive to be the best in everything. You should remain a virgin till the day you get married, or if you never get married, you should go to your grave a virgin. I am telling you the truth. With teenaged boys, sex is the most important thing on their brains. They will tell you they love you and in order for you to prove your love for them, they will ask you for sex. Teenagers, please listen to me, if you allow these young boys to have sex with you, you will be just another notch on their belt. I am not saying that all boys conduct themselves in this manner, but many of them do.

After they have used you to fulfill their sexual appetite, they will move on to the next available girl. You will be left devastated and questioning why you could not keep that boyfriend. Nothing is wrong with you; you simply made yourself available to someone who lacked good values. It is for this reason that teenaged girls should set high standards and live by them. When you set high standards, the man that the Lord has for you will have the utmost respect for you. Your vows will not be taken lightly on your wedding day. Your spouse will respect, love, and cherish you, and the Lord will pour out His blessings upon your union. There will be no past relationship for your husband to hold against you.

I know of a pastor's daughter who, as a little girl, loved the Lord, lived for Him, and when she became a teenager she started listening to worldly music and desired to engage in worldly activities. At age nineteen, she decided to take a chance and slept with a young man from the church. That one time is all it took for her to become pregnant. You see, she took a chance. She did not think that anyone would find out, but everyone did. Her father, the pastor of the church, was very embarrassed. His daughter's conduct changed their lives dramatically. The pregnant girl got married to the young man and she had to quit school to raise their daughter. Her husband, being a young man without an education, had to take jobs that paid minimum wage. This is not the life God intended for her, or for that young man for that matter. All it takes is one mistake.

Teenagers reading this: there is a time and place for everything. Now is the time for you to enjoy your teenaged years. Spend time with friends who will influence you in a positive manner. Learn about God's words, and His plan for your lives. He will enable you to endure until marriage.

YOUNG WOMEN AND UNMARRIED WOMEN

Young women, when people are looking for good qualities in you, what do you think they are looking for? People are looking for honesty, kindness, gentleness, warmth, one that is able to forgive and move on, a hard worker, and a person who lives uprightly. These are some of the traits that people look for when they want to hire you, when they want to date you, and when they want to marry you.

Always be honest in everything you do. Try to be kind-hearted, gentle, caring, loving toward others, and always put your best foot forward in all that you do. You see, you do not know who is looking at you and for what reason. I was promoted on one of my jobs without even applying for the promotion. The job was simply given to me. After I started the new position, I was told by a colleague of mine that the reason she recommended me for the promotion was because of the way I talked and got along with all my colleagues, and the fact that for every deadline, I was always the first to accomplish my assigned tasks.

Unmarried women, this chapter is for you also. Why aren't you married? Is it by choice or because you have not found the right person yet? Are you too picky and choosy, so that even if the right husband is out there for you, you let him slip by because of your pickiness? If you choose not to get married, that is acceptable. However, if you want to be married and you notice that no one is coming around, check yourself. First of all, are you praying and asking God to send you a godly man? That must be the first thing you ask God for—a godly man, the man that God has for you. I have seen so many women marry men who are not God-fearing men, and they end up miserable. They are miserable because of a choice they made instead of allowing God to make the choice for them.

MARRIED WOMEN

Many of us marry men who are not Christians, or we became Christians after getting married, but our husbands are not yet Christians. It is not easy wanting to live the way God wants us to live when our husbands are not saved. Nevertheless, God will help us. Those of us who are married, how do we know if we are virtuous or not? Are we the wives who put God first in everything? Do we say, "Oh, my husband wants me to cuddle tonight, so I cannot go to church"? Yet, when we were looking for a husband, we were in church every night? How do we speak to our husbands? Do we answer them back roughly when we do not get our way? Do we withhold sex from them when we want them to do things for us? Do we still prepare nice meals, and keep our homes clean? Do we possess the same personality that we had before we got married, or have we changed? Are we the bosses in the homes? Do we want to control our husbands?

The Bible tells us that the husband is the head of our homes, so we must let them be the head. Of course, you should not allow your husband to abuse you; I am saying that the man is the head of the household and he has to answer to God for all he does as the authority figure in the home. He is responsible for providing for his wife and children, and for the spiritual aspects of his household. Therefore, he has to give account to God.

Women, we must do our part in raising virtuous women in our homes, our churches, our schools, and our communities. We must pray for our teenaged girls, our young adults, and our married women. It is not easy to be a virtuous woman with all the temptations in our present society, but if we teach our daughters, sisters, aunts, cousins, and friends how to be virtuous, the Lord will help us to maintain our virtue. Always remember, we do not know who is looking at us, but we know that God is always looking at us, so let us live to please God. Let us train ourselves and our young women to be holy, upright, and pure—to be like Mary, Jesus' mother, a virtuous woman.

12
A Man's Virtue

When I began writing this book, I thought it was to be written for women, to discuss women issues, but the Lord impressed upon my heart that the teenaged boys, the young adult males, the unmarried and married men, Christian and non-Christian can benefit from what God wants to teach them. Men, listen up. What I am about to tell you will change your life, it will change your destiny, and if one man's life is saved, delivered, and set free, then it will be worth it.

TEENAGE BOYS

Let me begin with teenaged boys. I have a nineteen –year-old son named Gregory. Gregory gave his heart to the Lord when he was around seven years old. I praise God for Greg; he has been obedient. He respects his parents, his peers, his elders, and he is a decent young man. I thank God for his life. However, lately, since becoming nineteen, I noticed that he is more interested in girls.

Do not get me wrong, I know that at age nineteen his behaviour is normal. Nevertheless, I still want him to balance his interest and allow God to direct his decisions.

You see, the standard I have for Kristin is the same standard I have for Greg. I see so many young teenaged boys, those I taught since they were in elementary school, those living in my neighbourhood, and sons of the many relatives and friends I have, who end up on the wrong track.

Unfortunately, I have seen these innocent lives wasted. Some of these teenagers are behind bars, some are on drugs, and some are having sex with everything in a skirt.

Regrettably, some of these teenaged boys do not have fathers as their role models. They see the rappers on television and the gangsters around their neighbourhood— these are the people these boys want to fashion their lives after. The majority of teen-aged boys just want to "score" with the girls, and they do not care who they hurt, or what disease they get. All that matters is that they are having sex. Some of these bright young boys who had so much potential when they were in elementary school are now wandering the streets without knowing where to go or what to do.

It is essential for young men to treat young women with re-spect. I told my son that he has to treat girls with respect. He knows that God will provide a wife for him, but he has to pray for that Godly wife, one that knows the Lord as her Saviour. If you are a teenaged boy reading this book, I will tell you the same things I told my own son. I know some of your mothers have told you the same things: "Don't do drugs, don't drink, and don't bring any babies home for me to take care of." I will not reiterate that, because by now you are already fed up of hearing the same advice over and over again. What I will tell you is that Jesus loves you and that God has a plan and a purpose for your life. In order to fulfill your divine destiny, you have to accept Jesus as your Lord and Saviour, you have to pray without ceasing—pray for your life as if there is no tomorrow—and you have to fight for what you want. When I say fight, I mean fight. It is a spiritual battle you have to fight and the only way you can do this is to pray, and press on until you win the war.

You see, the war is against satan. satan does not want to see any of you young men live for the Lord, much less fulfill God's plan for your lives. satan will plant disrespect and stubbornness in you. He will also sew seeds of rebellion, mischief, and impurity in you. When this happens, you will behave in strange ways. That is when you will feel like taking a drink or trying drugs. You will experiment with sexual activity, and even engage in intercourse with other boys. This is how it all begins, and you know that you will end up either hooked or dead, which will eventually lead you to Hell.

My mother told me, "All that glitters isn't gold." It simply means that what looks good on the outside is not necessarily good on the inside. Sometimes you may see a girl who appears to be extremely attractive, but let me tell you something young men… satan has his agents, and sometimes these agents are disguised as young girls. They are sent to tempt young boys and they are used to lure them into satan's trap.

I once read a book in which the author was taken to Hell by God for forty days. The Lord showed her visions of Hell and asked her to write about it. She said that when God took her into Hell, she saw an old woman, all wrinkled up, who suddenly changed into a young teenaged girl. Then she changed into a young adult, before transforming into a grown woman, and then finally an old wrinkled woman again. The author said God told her that while this woman was alive, she was an agent of satan. She was able to attract teenaged boys by transforming into a beautiful teenaged girl. When she wanted an older man, she would transform into an older woman. So there in Hell, she kept burning and transforming eternally.

I mention this because I want you teenaged boys to know that you may see a nice looking girl and you may think that you have to be with her. But be careful: you could be sleeping with one of satan's agents. You could be having sex with a witch, and once you have sex with a witch, you become entangled in her demonic trap. Your life will become hers, and you may never have control of your life again. You will begin to notice that you no longer have the zeal to do the things of God, and you will not accomplish the goals that you had originally set out to accomplish.

Teenaged boys, do not allow satan to rob you of your life, your joy, your peace, and your happiness. Now is the time to accept Christ as your Lord and Saviour. If you are a Christian, now is the time to return to God and really tell Him how much you love Him, ask for His forgiveness, and ask God to direct your life. Whether you are a Christian or not, now is the time to dedicate your life to God and ask Him to direct your path.

Be aware that the temptations out there are real. They are there to divert your destiny and keep you away from the accomplishments that God has for you. When God blesses you with the right girl who is to become your wife, you will know it. She will be the best girl ever, and you will love her from your heart, not your head. You will know for sure that she is the right one for you. Without praying, and without depending on God, you will end up going from girlfriend to girlfriend, you will be left dissatisfied and empty. This is not what God intends for your life.

I know it is difficult, especially when you are among your peers who are all boasting about their accomplishments. For fear of looking stupid, you smoke, drink, take drugs, and live promiscuous lifestyles. I am here to tell you today that, no matter what, you should be yourself. Many of you are battling this inside. You know who you are, and you know that you are really not that kind of a young man, yet you give in to peer pressure.

Listen, God wants you for you. You, as an individual, must stand out for Jesus. When you stand up and stand out for Jesus, the Lord will take you to greater heights for Him, heights that you cannot imagine. So many of you have great dreams of becoming the next big star, but you must be the bright star that God intended for you to be. Shine for Jesus; let your light shine so that others may know about Jesus Christ and what He has done for you. Get involved in church activities and be a part of the youth group. All these things will teach you, direct you, and bless you. Who knows, you might find that special girl who God has chosen to be your wife at one of these church events or youth groups. My prayer for every teenaged boy reading this book is that God's plans for your life will be fulfilled.

Recently, I spoke to a friend of mine who is married to a minister. She mentioned to me that her sixteen-year-old son, who was raised in the church, is now staying away from church and questioning God. My heart sank when my friend told me about her son, because he is such a quiet, decent, loving child. I have known this young boy since childhood, and I have always known him to love going to church and serving God. Over the years, he became ill with different sicknesses which prevented him from taking part in sports. He really enjoyed playing sports. He started questioning why God allowed negative things to happen to His people, and over time he stopped going to church. Now, this young man sits at home and watches television, plays games, and hangs out with non-Christian friends.

It is not easy to live the Christian life. If anyone tells you that it is easy, they are lying to you. You see, it is only by God's grace that Christians can endure. The reason I say this is that once you are living for the Lord, satan will always try to discourage you; he will always put stumbling blocks along your path. I heard a pastor once say that if you are a Christian and you do not have any problems, check yourself, because it is only when you are living for the Lord that satan troubles you. If you are on satan's side, he will just leave you there to die. He will only give you enough rope to hang yourself with, as the saying goes. So if you are reading this book and you are a teenaged Christian boy, know that you are targeted by satan.

What causes a Christian to doubt all he has learned about God since he was an infant? It is sad, very sad, but it is the lies of the devil. satan whispers in the ears of our youth, and causes them to turn away from God. When our prayers have not been answered, satan tells us that God does not care about us. If our teenaged boys are not grounded, praying daily, reading God's Word daily, satan will be able to plot against them.

You will be tried, tempted, and tried again and again, but it is not worth giving up your salvation for the pleasures of the world. All the "blings" in the world are not worth going after if it means you will not make it into Heaven. *Heaven is real, and Hell is real.* No matter what the devil may throw at you, fight the fight of faith, and really trust God. Believe that Jesus is always at your right side and that the Lord has sent His angels to encamp around you. All you have to do is ask your angel to fight for you, and hold on to what you know about Jesus.

My prayer is that all the Christian teenaged boys who once knew the Lord and lived for Him will one day soon return to Him. Tomorrow you may be dead and find yourself in Hell, so do not wait. Ask God to forgive you and fill you with His Spirit and His love. When you devote your life to Christ, you will be too hot for satan to handle. In other words, satan will try, but it will be difficult for him to succeed.

For the unsaved teenaged boys, please note that there is no guarantee for tomorrow. Tomorrow does not belong to you; tomorrow belongs to God. You don't know if you will live to see tomorrow, so decide today to accept the Lord Jesus Christ as your Lord and Saviour. By giving your life to Jesus, and by living for Him, you will be guaranteed to make it into Heaven, and while on earth you will be protected, you will be blessed, and God's plans for your life will be fulfilled. Don't let satan rob you of what God has in store for your life.

YOUNG UNMARRIED MEN

Let me speak directly now to the young unmarried men.

Some of you think that you are in the prime of your lives and that you have the rest of your lives to find Jesus. Some of you like to dress to impress, and there is nothing wrong with that. A brother must look good, I agree. Some of you have been hurt by young women. Some are battling with what to study, where to study, what career path to take, what car to buy, what girl to fool tonight, and how to know which woman to choose for a bride. Others are simply thinking about the next party, and the next superficial moment of pleasure.

Young men, have you ever thought of the kinds of girls you date? Are these the kinds of girls you could see yourself taking home to your parents to say, "Hi mom and dad, this is Marie, I would like to marry her"? Have you guys really looked deep inside and asked yourselves, "Why am I dating this girl? Is it for sex, for a fun time, to look good because she looks good, or is it because I really care and love this girl?"

How many of you guys really know what love is? Have you ever really felt love? Where, in your head or in your heart? I keep saying this because many of you young men fall into traps. There are many traps that the devil sets for young men. On many occasions, I have heard of bright young men whose lives and destinies were changed because they "had to marry" their girlfriend. That's right, "had to marry." Why? Because she was pregnant and they were forced to marry her!

I have met so many young men in my life whose lives have been altered by young women who just want to have a good time. They do not have a care in the world about their soul and where they will end up. There are some women out there who satan uses just to have sex with young men. That is what we call "sex demons." Have you ever been with a girl and all she wants to do is have sex all the time? Sometimes after having sex with you over and over again in one night, she still wants more. Maybe you think, "Oh, she's great in bed, wow!" But that is not it. On many occasions, these women are demonized. When you have sex with women like these, they share their demonic seeds with you. That is why it is so important not to sleep around with anyone before you are married.

I know that you have heard about HIV and the many other diseases prevalent in today's society. Therefore, I will not reiterate it. I am here to educate you about the spiritual things that take place when you have sex with women. First of all, for every person you sleep with, whether male or female, you are joined spiritually with them. So just imagine, if she slept with twenty men throughout her life, she is bringing twenty different spirits with her—once you both are joined sexually, that will make it twenty-one spirits that you have to live with and deal with.

Listen carefully. May the Lord Jesus Christ open your eyes and ears to what I am telling you. Young men, if you have had sex with girls or boys, ask God to forgive you, and recall every time you had sex, recall it in the Spirit, and ask God to destroy every evil deposit that was left in you because of that sex act. If you have never had sex before, thank God. Do not start. Just ask God to keep you pure until you are married.

satan is real. You must be thinking by now that every chapter in this book speaks about satan. Well, the title of the book is *The Silent Death*. I am here to warn you of the silent ways and tricks that satan uses to kill you. Having sex before marriage is wrong, and the Bible tells us so: *"For this is the will of God, even your sanctification, that ye should abstain from fornication"* (1 Thessalonians 4:3). Having sex before marriage could kill you both physically and spiritually.

THINGS TO LOOK FOR IN WOMEN

Respect breeds respect. Therefore, young men, when you are looking for a life mate, look for a woman who is kind and gentle. Do not look for a woman who is controlling or bossy. The qualities you should look for in a woman are as follows: she should be kind, gentle, loving, forgiving, pure, holy, respectable, and most of all able to be content despite the circumstances that she is faced with. Best of all, she should know the Lord Jesus Christ as her personal Saviour, and she must be living for the Lord wholeheartedly.

First of all, you must look for a woman who is God-fearing. She must be a Christian woman who spends time reading the Bible and praying. She should be one who obeys God. She must also be a woman who pays her tithes and is a giver. The reason I say this is because if you find a woman who does these things—reads her Bible, spends quality time praying, pays her tithes, gives, and obeys God—you know that she will be committed to you as well.

You see, if a woman puts God first, you know that she is being directed by God. If she reads the Word of God and prays about things before she does them, you know that she is a patient woman; she will not be the type to be in haste.

The Bible tells us to *"honour the Lord with thy substance, and with the firstfruits of all thine increase"* (Proverbs 3:9). If a woman honours God with her substance, if she pays her tithes, you know that she is a blessed woman. In other words, if the woman you are seeking is a giver, you know that God's blessings will be poured out upon her, and ultimately upon you.

Secondly, the woman's character should show that she is respectful. I know of a man who was married previously, but the marriage did not work out. He had children with different women, but finally settled down and lived in a common-law relationship with a woman. The woman was attractive, she kept the house spotlessly clean, she did his laundry, and did an excellent job at raising his children. Although she did all these good things, she disrespected him in front of his family and friends. I could see sometimes that he wished the earth could open up so that he could hide. All her good deeds did not compensate for her disrespectful nature, and in the end, he left her.

THE SILENT DEATH

MARRIED MEN—CHRISTIAN AND NON-CHRISTIAN

Many of you have been married for years, but you have noticed your marriages deteriorating. Your decisions to get married were influenced by a variety of things: you were madly in love, your lady friend was pregnant, you were pressured by your peers, your marriage was prearranged from birth, or you couldn't decide which of your many lady friends to marry so you chose a wife randomly.

Brothers, there is a difference when you pray and ask God to provide a wife for you. When God gives you a wife, he gives you the best. God gives you your soul mate, your life partner, the one who will stick with you through thick and thin. If you lean on your own understanding in choosing a wife, you will make terrible mistakes.

If you already chose a wife, whether you are a Christian man or not, listen up. Your wife desires to be loved, cherished, put on a pedestal, and respected. Women also like to receive flowers and gifts. If a woman tells you, "Oh, you don't need to buy me any flowers or anything," she is probably not being completely truthful. Ninety-nine percent of the women I know love to receive flowers.

When was the last time you bought your wife flowers? You might be saying, "I don't have any money, things are tight, and I am the only provider in this home; where would I have money to buy flowers?" Believe me, buy your wife flowers and see how it brightens her day. The other day, my son bought me a flowerpot with daisies in it, and it surely brightened my day. It was a reminder that he appreciates me. Imagine how I would have felt had my husband given me those flowers! He does on occasion.

Many men, when they are dating, show the women their best, and the women do the same. They take their fiancé out to the movies and shows, buy her gifts and flowers, and talk to her nicely, trying their best not to let their "bad side" show even when they are furious. Sadly enough, as soon as the ring goes on her finger, the true nature of both individuals begins to show.

There are some of you who allow your parents, your brothers and sisters, and friends and relatives to control how you treat your wives. So many marriages have in-law problems. The Bible tells us that a man must leave his mother and father's house and cleave to his wife. How many of you are still a Mama's boy? How many of you, when your wife cooks for you, you leave the food and go to your mother's to eat? How many of you will buy the best gift for your mother and give your wife something that is just an afterthought? How many of you know that you are con-sciously treating your wife like a second-class citizen, or worse?

How many of you love your wife with all your heart? How many of you cheat on your wives without feeling guilty about it? How many of you pray with your wife on a daily basis? How many of you cherish, honour, and respect your wives for all that she does? Remember, your wife does not have to be working out-side the home to be considered a hard-working woman. I am speaking from experience. It is harder to cook, clean, care for the children, and have energy to make love to your husband than it is to go to work outside the home.

Married men, this is a wake-up call. The Lord is directing me to tell you that the woman you chose as your wife needs your love. Pray with and for her, appreciate her, listen to her, and read between the lines sometimes. Sometimes it is not what she says— at times, you need to focus on what she does not say. You need to be aware when she is hurting, know when she is tired, know when she is just holding on by a thread, and do something about it. I am telling you, if a woman is being treated poorly at home, satan is there to tempt her, and many of your wives will find love, understanding, patience, kindness, and support elsewhere.

Whether you are a teenaged boy, a young unmarried man, a married man, Christian or not, I hope the information the Holy Spirit provided for you will guide you to be the best you can be. I hope my advice will direct the teenagers in the right path. I pray that the unmarried men will really pray and ask God to provide for them the wife that God has for them. It is only who God chooses for you that will last.

For the married Christians and the non-Christians, I trust that you have learned something about women and how we really feel. I am praying that the Lord will continue to bless and keep your marriages, and that there will be greater understanding, love, and togetherness. If you allow the Lord to be first in your lives, in your marriages, in your homes, and in your decisions, only then will you be able to succeed. The trials will come, but by God's grace, He will see you through it. Temptations will come, but the Lord Jesus Christ will allow you to overcome them. Remember, in everything give God the praise, and if God put you two together, no man, no woman, no devil will be successful in breaking you apart. Trust God.

For the non-Christian married man, this is what the Lord is saying to you: Accept Jesus as your Lord and Saviour and put Him first. Ask God to forgive you of all your sins and look for a Spirit-filled church to go to. Dedicate your marriage to the Lord and sincerely and truly love your wife. Cherish her, bless her, and help her. I promise that if you do these things, God will bless you and you will have peace, love, joy, and happiness in your home.

When temptations come, when battles come, the Lord will fight for you and you will have the victory!

13
Obedience to God

As a teacher, I expect my students to be obedient to me. They must be well-behaved and well-prepared for class at all times. As a parent, I also expect my children to listen to me and obey. But when it comes to God, how many of us really obey Him? I am a prime example of a person who has not been obedient to God. The Lord asked me to write this book in 1999, and I procrastinated. I am now completing it in 2009.

Indeed, we all think that we are obedient to God. However, we do the things He asks us to do in our own time, and we consider such actions obedient. According to the Concise Oxford Dictionary, "obedience" means to *submit to another's rule or to comply with a law or command."*[3] When God asks us to do something, we should obey right away and do it.

---

[3] *The Concise Oxford Dictionary (8th Edition).* Oxford University Press, New York, 1990. p.816

I know firsthand that it is not always easy to obey God. What makes us disobey Him? Is it fear, anxiety, or lack of knowledge? Or perhaps some of us feel that we have all the time in the world to get things done for God. However, if we do not get done what He wants accomplished, He will call someone else to do it for Him. We know that we were brought into this world for a purpose, and before we leave here, many of us may not fulfill God's purpose in our lives. Many of us missed our breakthroughs and our blessings in life because we did not obey God.

If the Lord calls you to be a pastor and you diddle and daddle, it means you are not complying with His command. It means that you are disobeying God. Many people go to universities and colleges to study the Word of God, but this education is no substitute for the calling of God. If your reason for becoming a pastor is that you think you'll have it easy, drive fancy cars, and own big homes, then you need to think again. If the Lord *calls* you to be a pastor, be one. The Lord will equip you to be the best pastor ever. If the Lord did not call you to become a pastor, ask God for direction, and obey.

The Bible tells us about the Ten Commandments in Exodus 20. Some of us have read this scripture over and over again, while many of us have never heard of these commandments. For those who have not heard of the Ten Commandments, here they are (from Exodus 20):

1. Thou shalt have no other gods before me.
2. Thou shalt not make unto thee any graven image, or any likeness of any thing that is in heaven above or that is in the earth beneath, or that is in the water under the earth: thou shalt not bow down thyself to them, nor serve them: for I the Lord thy God am a jealous god, visiting the in-

iquity of the fathers upon the children unto the third and fourth generation of them that hate me; and shewing mercy unto thousands of them that love me, and keep my commandments.

3. Thou shalt not take the name of the Lord thy God in vain; for the Lord will not hold him guiltless that taketh his name in vain.

4. Remember the sabbath day, to keep it holy. Six days shalt thou labour, and do all thy work: but the seventh day is the sabbath of the Lord thy God: in it thou shalt not do any work, thou, nor thy son, nor thy daughter, thy manservant, nor thy maidservant, nor thy cattle, nor the stranger that is within thy gates: For in six days the Lord made heaven and earth, the sea, and all that in them is, and rested the seventh day: wherefore the Lord blessed the sabbath day, and hallowed it.

5. Honour thy father and thy mother: that thy days may be long upon the land which the Lord thy God giveth thee.

6. Thou shalt not kill.

7. Thou shalt not commit adultery.

8. Thou shalt not steal.

9. Thou shalt not bear false witness against thy neighbour.

10. Thou shalt not covet thy neighbour's house, thou shalt not covet thy neighbour's wife, nor his manservant, nor his maidservant, nor his ox, nor his ass, nor anything that is thy neighbour's.

LOVE THE LORD, NOT IDOLS

The Ten Commandments began with the Lord saying to put Him first, and avoid all other Gods. By putting God first in every area of our lives, the Lord will direct us, and He will give us understanding. Matthew 6:33 states, *"But seek ye first the kingdom of God, and his righteousness; and all these things shall be added unto you."* Once we put God first in every situation and in every aspect of our lives, we will not be disappointed.

The commandments also tell us to *avoid false gods.* Many people worship false gods without being aware of what they are doing. Although we may not worship a cow, the moon, or a statue, many of us give our hundred percent attention to material things. Such things are considered false gods.

For example, some people put money before God. They commit more time to earning money than to worshipping God. Unfortunately, all the money one makes in his lifetime will not give you peace, joy, or the happiness that comes with putting God first and living for Him.

Some of us worship movie stars and athletes. I know of some people who have their favourite stars' pictures up on their walls and they talk to the pictures daily before leaving their homes. Nevertheless, when you idolize people, they will disappoint you. After all, they are only human.

Many people stay home from church on Sundays to wash their vehicles and to watch the football game on television. Their focus is on things that can only provide temporary fulfillment, which is why so many people are bored and fed up with their lives. Instead of having the Holy Spirit in them, they use material things to fill that void.

So many people worship idols in some form or another. However, based on the second commandment of the living God, worshiping idols is wrong. The Bible tells us that our God is a jealous God, and if you are worshiping idols instead of Him, He will punish you and your generations to come.

Let us not forget this great Commandment: to love the Lord with all our hearts, our souls, and our might. Remember to put God first and everything else will be added unto us.

REVERE THE LORD'S NAME

The Lord admonishes us not to use His name in vain. Our words have power. The words we speak can either bless or curse, so we must be very careful of what comes out of our mouths. So many of us use the Lord's name in vain. For example, when we stumble and bump our foot, we say things like, "Oh God, Oh God, Oh God, my foot hurts!" This is using God's name in vain and it is wrong. We must remember to use God's name reverently, because one day we will have to give an account for it.

THE SABBATH DAY

In the fourth commandment, we are told to observe the Sabbath day. We should not work, but worship the Lord and rest on this day. I can hear all the screaming going on even as I discuss this commandment. You are probably questioning, "What does she mean when she says not to work on Sundays? How am I going to pay my bills?"

I know how important it is to have to work and pay your bills, rent and mortgages, but the Bible tells us that the Lord created seven days, six to work and on the seventh, we must rest and worship Him. The seventh day belongs to the Lord Jesus Christ. This is a day that we should meet with God, spend time with Him, and commune with Him. The Lord promised that if we do that, He will provide for us.

Obedience to God

Honour Your Parents

For those of you who have your mothers and fathers alive, be thankful. If you have not been honouring them, ask God to forgive you and start now. For some reason, many young people today believe they do not have to honour or obey their parents. The Bible tells us that we must honour our parents, and the Lord will give us long life.

Do Not Kill

The Lord gives life and He is the only one responsible for taking it away from us. When we have abortions, when we commit suicide, and when we kill our brothers and sisters, we have broken His commandment. If you are in a position where you are guilty of murder, ask God to forgive you and He will pardon your sin.

I realize that many of us view suicide as our only option to end misery in our lives. Before I accepted Jesus, when I was going through rough times in my life, the thought of committing suicide crossed my mind on many occasions. satan tempted me to crash my car while traveling on the highway, but praise be to God, I did not go through with it. Some Christians today think of committing suicide. I am here to tell you, it is wrong, and it is only Jesus who can destroy the spirit that encourages you to take your life.

In today's society, killing is glamorized by television shows, movies, and video games. You may think that it is a cool thing to go in front of your peers and kill someone. However, this is a lie that satan tells us. He then leaves us alone to defend ourselves after we commit the crime.

If you have ever killed anyone, ask God to forgive you. You may be in jail right now reading this book, but it is not too late to ask God for forgiveness. The Lord God Almighty will forgive you. After you have asked God to forgive you, accept Jesus as your Lord and Saviour. Ask Jesus to come into your heart and live in you. Brothers and sisters, you will see the difference. You will see what God will do in your lives. He will amaze you!

ADULTERY

The Bible tells us that we should not commit adultery; it is a sin. So many married men and women commit this sin and they think that it is all right to do it over and over again, because they believe their wife or husband does not know they are having an affair.

There is no excuse for anyone to commit adultery. When a man and woman make a vow before God, and they promise to be faithful to each other, no matter what, that man and woman should remain faithful in that marriage. I can hear some of you men saying, "But have you seen my wife? That is not the sexy woman I married ten years ago!" And I can hear you women saying, "He treats me so badly, that this is revenge. What he doesn't know won't hurt him. If he had been treating me well, I wouldn't have to look outside for love."

Whichever way you look at it, whatever excuse you may think you have, committing adultery is wrong. The Bible says in Hebrews 13:4 that *"marriage is honourable in all, and the bed unde-filed: but whoremongers and adulterers God will judge."* In other words, the husband should represent God in his home. The man is responsible for the wellbeing of his wife and children. If a man commits adultery, he is not upholding his promise to "have and to hold, in sickness and in health." The same goes for a woman if she commits adultery. Both shall be judged.

Obedience to God

How can you expect your children to respect you? How can you look at yourselves in the mirror and honestly justify what you have done? There is no justification that will satisfy your guilt. This act will only cause you more grief, more sorrow, and it will ultimately lead to your destruction.

I know that there are temptations out there, but be strong. Ask the Lord to take the temptations away from you, and to strengthen you. I promise you that when the urge comes to commit adultery, the Lord Jesus Christ will take it away.

You may have committed adultery on numerous occasions. Just ask God for forgiveness, ask your wife or your husband for forgiveness, and seek counselling if you have to; but don't stay in your situation. If you remain in your situation, you will end up depressed, diseased, or even dead, so hearken unto this warning and stop what you are doing. Your wife or your husband may not know what you have done, but God knows. In the end, you will have to give an account to God for all your actions.

Do Not Steal

How many of us have stolen small items at work, like notepads, pencils, and pens? Though these items are small, your act of stealing is very significant in the eyes of God. In our minds, we limit stealing to robbing a bank or stealing a car. However, stealing is simply taking things that do not belong to you. The Bible tells us that we must not steal. It is a sin, so please abstain from stealing and obey God's commandment.

Do Not Lie

Telling lies is a sin and God despises a liar. So many of us tell a little lie here and there, thinking that God will ignore it, but He cannot ignore it because He cannot defy His own Word. According to the Bible, the truth will set you free. Ask the Holy Spirit to control your mouth, so that you will always tell the truth.

COVETING

When you covet, you strongly desire something that does not belong to you. This passion to have that "thing" can drive you to commit heinous crimes. The Bible tells us that this is a sin. Always be grateful for what you have, and be thankful for what you don't have. Know that God is in control, and when He is ready to bless you, He will, all in His time.

This chapter dealt with obeying God. In order to obey God, you must know about the Laws of God, which is why I included the Ten Commandments. The Ten Commandments are not to be taken lightly. They are God's rules for our lives. The Lord God Almighty gave us these rules so that we would not commit sin so that we can make it into Heaven. If we follow God's rules, we will reap tremendous benefits, not only on Earth, but also in Heaven and throughout eternity.

14
Salvation Is No Joke!

What is Salvation? Salvation is when you accept the Lord Jesus Christ as your Lord and Saviour. It means that you are saved. To be saved means that you now belong to Jesus Christ; you no longer belong to the devil. Salvation is the most important step in your life. It is the step you take to ensure that your name is written in the Lamb's Book of Life. It is the decision you make to guarantee your place in Heaven.

So many of us take our salvation lightly. When Jesus was crucified on that cross over two thousand years ago, He did it for you and me. Jesus sacrificed His life in order for us to have everlasting life. In order for us to have everlasting life with Him in Heaven, we must first accept Jesus into our hearts as our Lord and Saviour.

How many of you reading this book have not accepted Jesus Christ as your Lord and Saviour? How many of you have heard about Jesus and are just waiting for the right day and time to accept Him? How many of you know you need Jesus in your life, but yet think you can make it without Him? How many of you believe that Jesus will never change you or your situation? How many of you hang onto your religious beliefs and your family's traditions? How many of you know the truth, that Jesus died on the cross, rose from the dead, and is coming back again, yet you pretend you do not believe Jesus is coming back again?

You may have heard about Jesus all your life, yet you ignored all that you have heard and seen. I am here today to tell you that you cannot pretend anymore. You cannot say, "I'll give my heart to the Lord tomorrow." I know of so many people who have made this promise, yet died before fulfilling their commitment. You cannot ignore the fact that Jesus Christ is the son of God. He died, rose from the dead, and is coming back again. You and I cannot live our lives any old way anymore because Jesus is coming back for us, and we have to give an account to Him as to how we lived our lives. If God is not pleased, we will go to Hell for eternity. There is no turning back.

Hell is real. Do not let anyone fool you into thinking that Hell is not real. The Bible tells us in 1 Thessalonians 5:9, *"For God hath not appointed us to wrath, but to obtain salvation by our Lord Jesus Christ."* This means that God does not want us to end up in Hell. He wants everyone to obtain salvation, so that we will be saved from eternal fire.

When you accept Jesus as your Lord and Saviour, your life will change instantly. Your destiny will change. Your place of everlasting rest will change. In other words, the plans that satan has for your life will change. When you open your heart and let Jesus come in, you are telling satan that you no longer belong to him. You are telling that old devil that now you are a child of God.

You have been bought by the precious blood of Jesus Christ and now Jesus is responsible for you and for your soul.

As I mentioned before, when you accept Jesus Christ as your Lord and Saviour, your name is automatically written down in His Book of Life. However, if you do not accept Jesus as your Lord and Saviour, your name will not be written in that book, and you will go to Hell. Where do you want to end up, Heaven or Hell? The choice is yours, and today you have to make that choice. Not tomorrow or next week or next year, because tomorrow, next week, or next year may be too late.

You may say to me, why is it that Christians struggle so much? I am here to tell you that when you accept Jesus Christ, life will not always be easy. satan will harass you more than ever. satan is happy when you are living for him, and he disguises the traps he sets for you.

satan has some people so hooked on gambling that they end up losing their homes, their marriages, their jobs... everything. satan has others hooked on brothels, ultimately leading to diseases like AIDS. When you get into trouble, end up in jail, or even dead, satan rejoices, because you will end up in his kingdom—a place where there is eternal fire and everlasting torture.

There are two choices: either you live for satan and end up in Hell or you accept Jesus Christ as your Lord and Saviour and live eternally in Heaven, where you will be at peace and have everlasting joy. Heaven is a place where you will walk and talk with God for eternity.

If you choose to continue living your life without God, without direction, and without purpose, it means you have chosen to live for satan, and you *will end up in Hell!*

If you choose to change your status from Hell to *HEAVEN*, it means that you have decided to follow Jesus. If you have decided to follow Jesus Christ, please pray the following prayer with me: "Father, in the name of Jesus, I love you. I ask you to forgive me of all my sins, and I accept the Lord Jesus Christ as my Lord and Saviour. Please Jesus, come into my heart right now. Live in me. In Jesus' name I pray, Amen."

If you have accepted Jesus Christ today, praise God! I urge you to find a spirit-filled church to attend, because now is when you will need to learn more about Jesus, be around other Christians who will help you in your walk with Christ.

BACKSLIDING

For those of you that have strayed from your Christian walk, I am not here to judge you at all. I am here to remind you of where you came from and what God has done for you. Remember, before you gave your heart to the Lord, how easy things seemed to come to you, and how empty you felt sometimes, as if something was missing? You know that on many occasions, when things were "given" to you so easily and unconditionally, you ended up in trouble. You ended up committing sin, and the happiness lasted only a short time.

You were once eager to read your Bible. You were excited to pray and to go to church, until one day maybe someone from the church said something to you that was not so nice, or maybe the pastor did not agree with something you did, or maybe it was you who wanted to continue in your way of life and could not adhere to the "rules" of being a Christian. Whatever it was, do not allow satan to lie to you. Do not allow satan to rob you of what God has planned for you. Do not permit the enemy of your soul to direct you back to his lifestyle, which will ultimately lead you to Hell.

Now is not the time to be doubting. Now is not the time to be debating if you should live for Jesus or go back to your old way of life. Now is not the time to play games with your life and with your destiny. You know for a fact, and it is true, that *Jesus is coming back again!* You know, this fact is real, so why procrastinate? Why play with your life? Do not think that you have tomorrow, for tomorrow does not belong to you; it belongs to God, and God can take your tomorrow away from you.

I read somewhere about a young man who once knew the Lord. He went to church with his family all his life, then suddenly he changed. He started going to clubs with his friends. One night, he went to a club and, because he was not drinking, he was the designated driver. After the party was over, he drove his friends home. While going home, he got into an accident and died instantly. Where do you think he ended up? Although he once accepted Christ, he denied Christ and it was in his time of denying Christ that he died.

I am writing to remind you that satan will use different situations to lie to you, to rob you, to divert your destiny away from what God wants for you. Please ask God to forgive you right now. Our God is a loving, forgiving God. Just sincerely say, "Father, forgive me, Jesus forgive me, and come into my heart. I love you." It is as simple as that. Return to Jesus, humble yourself, and do it. In the long run you will be victorious!

So many of us think that the Lord does not answer our prayers. We think He caused us to be in debt or get sick. I am here to tell you that sometimes, I too felt as if I was at the bottom of the barrel. But guess what? Sometimes we go through experiences in order to prove the mighty power of God. It is only through those hard times and disappointments that we can truly see what Jesus can do for us. Take it from me, as hard as it may seem sometimes, it is only by the grace of God that we will make it. The Lord God Almighty promised to never leave us or forsake us. (Isaiah 43:2). What God promised us, we will receive. Forgive, and put your old ways, thoughts, doubts, and fears behind you. Get up, brush yourself off, and start afresh with the Lord. Return to Him, for tomorrow may be too late.

You may have heard this before, but I want you to hear it again: Your salvation is no joke, do not take it lightly, and do not take it for granted because tomorrow may never come. It may be too late!

15

Defeating satan's Plans for Your Life

In the same manner that our Loving Father has our destiny planned out for our lives, so too does satan. satan and his agents hold meetings annually, monthly, weekly, and daily concerning our lives. In those meetings, he decides who he will rob from, who he will inflict diseases upon, and who he will kill— just to mention a few. satan is no respecter of persons. He has a quota to fill in Hell and he will do all he has to do to get you and me there.

You may ask me, "How do you know what satan's plans are for my life?" Well, I don't know his plan for your life; however, I have seen how he has tried to implement his plans in my life. When we look at the pattern in our lives, some of us have certain patterns in our genealogy. For example, in my genealogy, one girl in every branch of my family tree gets pregnant out of wedlock.

Another example in my family line is that we only achieve up to a certain level in life, and after that nothing else gets accomplished... or if it is accomplished, there is always a serious struggle.

Many of us started out our lives rich, healthy, important, and prominent—but where did many of us end up? Lost, poor, insignificant, and unable to acquire much in life. This is not God's plans for our lives; this is satan's plan in operation.

In order to know satan's plans for your life, you must first check your life pattern. Check the pattern in your family line. Is it at a certain age that Christian boys turn away from Christ? I have a relative whose in-laws were all Christians; however, he noticed that the men in that family, who were Christians from birth, eventually turned away from Christ.

Another pattern you may notice in your life, or in your family line, is that of hardship and struggle. No matter what you do, you may pay your tithes, you always give an offering, you sow seeds at church, you always give to charities, you give to the homeless, and to various organizations, yet you struggle to get anything for yourself. This is the plan of satan. You always seem to go through hardship in order to acquire simple things. This is the plan of satan.

Looking over my life, I realize that I only stayed in a job for about five years, then something would cause me to move on to another job. This is a pattern. satan's pattern in our lives is no mistake. He strategizes and plots his schemes. satan makes sure that whatever it takes, he will destroy you. Knowing the fact that satan plans for your lives is the first step in defeating him. When you realize that things do not "just happen," you will know that it is satan's scheme to pull you down.

How many of you notice that women in your family cannot get married? There are so many beautiful, intelligent, God-fearing women who cannot seem to find a husband. I remember I was in a service once and the pastor called up a woman—this pastor is an anointed man of God; the Lord uses him to prophecy.

In this service, he called up a sister and he started to prophecy on her life. He told her that men are always drawn to her, but that in the spiritual realm, she was already married. In other words, whenever a prospective husband came to get to know her, he would be hindered and driven away in the spiritual realm. The pastor then prayed for this sister's deliverance.

So many of you are thinking, what is wrong with me? Why can't I get married? Do not fret yourself. It is not you; it is satan's plan that is working in your life. So many of you women have spirit husbands attached to you and you don't even know it. Many of you have dreams about sexual activity with handsome men. Note that these types of dreams are linked to spirit husbands. You need to seek God for Him to deliver you.

Children are also affected by satan's plans. Many children start off in life loving God, living for Him, before rebellion steps in. The things of the world seem more important than the beliefs they were brought up with. This causes friction in homes, resulting in children being on the streets, prostituting their bodies, gambling, and stealing to survive.

As I mentioned before, satan is no respecter of persons. He knows that his days are numbered and that the Lord Jesus Christ is coming soon, so he is doing his best to see how many lives he can destroy before his reign is over.

How do we defeat satan? The most important rule in defeating satan's plan for your life is *Salvation!* This is the most important requirement for defeating satan. When you say yes to Jesus

Christ, Jesus will cover you with His Blood. His Blood that was shed on Calvary's Cross was shed for you and me. By accepting Jesus as your Lord and Saviour, you are telling satan that you no longer belong to him. You now belong to Jesus and by being a child of God, the Lord will protect you. He promised to deliver you, He promised to bless you, and He promised to set you free. So no matter what satan's plans are for your life, the Lord Jesus Christ will provide a way of escape for you. Remember, satan was already defeated over two thousand years ago, but by accepting Jesus as your Lord and Saviour, you will acquire protection for your life.

The second method of defeating satan's plan for your life is *Fasting and Praying*. When we fast and pray, the Lord reveals things to us. He directs us as to what to do, where to turn, how to avoid situations, and how to get out of trouble. The Lord Jesus Christ shows us the traps that the devil sets for us, and He helps us to avoid those traps.

The third rule in order to defeat satan's plan for your life is to *Avoid Unfriendly Friends*. This may seem difficult, but it is not. When I say to avoid unfriendly friends, I mean there are people who you may call your friends, but if you allow the Lord to open your eyes, you will see the things they do to you in the spirit. You will see the backstabbing. You will hear the lies they say about you. You will see the traps they set for you. Ask the Lord to expose who they are, bring them before you, and help you to stay away from them. I am talking about Christians as well as non-Christians. Oh yes, there are Christian "unfriendly friends" as well. These are the ones you really have to be careful of.

The fourth rule in order to defeat satan's plan for your life is *Check Yourself Daily*. If you check yourself daily, you will know if you are reading God's words. You will know if you are spending quality time with the Lord. You will know if you are "playing church." That is, the Holy Spirit will convict you about praising the Lord in your loudest voice, and speaking in tongues so that your pastor and your brethren can hear you, yet in private you refrain from praying and reading the Bible outside of church hours.

Check yourself and make sure that you do not give satan an inroad into your life. Do not give satan an excuse to visit you or to have a hold on your life. If you are constantly in tune with God, if you are living the true Christian life, satan will know and it will be more difficult for him to penetrate you.

The fifth and final rule for you to follow in order to defeat satan's plan for your life is *Believe, Trust, and Wait on God.* In order for God's plans to be established in your life, you must believe in God, trust in Him, and wait on Him. If you are in constant communication with Jesus Christ, He will lead you in the path that you should go. Do not be too hasty to do things. Always wait on God to direct you. When you wait on God and follow His direction, you will fulfill God's plans for your life, and by fulfilling God's plans for your life you will fulfill your divine destiny!

16

Achieving God's Plan and Purpose for Your Life

Do you know what God's plans are for your life? Do you know what your purpose is for being on this Earth? How many of you really know the answers to these questions? For many years, I did not have a clue as to what I was brought into this world to do. I only realized a few years ago that, although I did various jobs and have specific qualifications—a Bachelor of Arts in English, a Bachelor of Education, experience as a Special Education Specialist and Reading Specialist—my purpose goes beyond these jobs and qualifications. I was brought here to enlighten, to comfort, and to help others who are unbelievers, doubters, and those who think they should live without having to give an account for their actions. I am here to tell you that, one day, we will all have to give our Father in Heaven an account of our lives. We will have to tell Him what we did for Him and how we used the gifts and talents that He gave us to enlarge His Kingdom.

I remember, about ten years ago, there was a grade eight student that I taught who told me there was no God, and that he believed that the Earth simply existed. I felt sad to hear that this young boy did not know God. He had never heard about God, and he believed that within the universe, things just happened.

Too many of us think that we merely exist, and whatever will be, will be. Why do we live our lives by chance? If we think we are here by chance and that we can live our lives anyway we want, we need to think again. We are not here by chance, and you must know that we were all created, you and me, for a purpose. The Lord brought us into this world with something special in mind. He has deposited good things in our lives and we are to accomplish what God brought us here to accomplish. So, to tell you the truth, you are not here by chance. You were born into this world for a purpose. It does not matter how you were conceived, whether through love, through revenge, through unplanned pregnancy, or through rape. What matters is that you were beautifully and wonderfully made by God and know that God has a plan and a purpose for your life. (Proverb 3:6)

In order to learn what God's plan is for your life, you have to pray to God for the answer. I cannot tell you what to do with your lives. In high schools, there are guidance counsellors who will tell you what to become in life based on your strengths. Sometimes they are right and sometimes they are very wrong. When you pray and ask God to reveal His purpose and His plan for your life, you know that you will never go wrong. The Lord may use people to confirm His plans for your life, but you are the one who has to seek His direction.

So many of you, like me, have done many jobs. We go from job to job, yet we know deep down that this is not where we ought to be, and we do nothing about it. Until you are where the Lord wants you to be, you will never be happy, you will not be satisfied, and you will always feel that something is missing.

I am speaking from experience. When I migrated to Canada, I worked for a travel agency. That was nice, but I knew that that was not where I had to be. Mind you, I was not a born again Christian then, but somehow I just knew that I was not going to be at the agency for the rest of my life. From there, I worked at a bank and with the federal government, both of which I enjoyed, but I knew there was more I had to accomplish. I later went back to university to obtain my Bachelor of Arts and Bachelor of Education degrees. As a teacher, I am fulfilling part of God's plan for my life.

This book, *The Silent Death*, is God's plan and purpose for my life. By writing about the Lord and telling others about accepting Jesus as their Lord and Saviour, and by telling millions of people about the traps of satan and the ways in which he can kill you and you don't know it, I am fulfilling my purpose in life. I am trusting that the Lord Jesus Christ will use this book to further His Kingdom and to accomplish in me what He wants to accomplish.

It is imperative that every believer and non-believer reading this book take the time to fast and pray about God's plan and purpose for their lives. I have heard of so many people whose lives have started out great but have ended up broke, lost, in prison, or dead, simply because they did their own thing, without depending on the Lord for direction. Do not wander from place to place, or from job to job, without a clue as to what you are meant to accomplish in this life.

In order to achieve God's plan and purpose for your life, you have to know Jesus as your Lord and Saviour. If you have not accepted Jesus as your Lord and Saviour, you should accept Him now. Once you are in tune with the Holy Spirit, the Holy Spirit will tell you where you have to go, what you have to accomplish, and how to accomplish God's plans for your life.

Many of us ought to be millionaires, yet we are still living our life in poverty. It could be a simple direction from the Lord that can change our situation and make us millionaires. I remember a crusade I once attended. At the crusade, there was a preacher from Nigeria. I remember him telling us that all it takes to change our destiny is to know God's will concerning our lives. He went on to say that there was a man in Nigeria who was a school principal. He was a born again Christian who paid his tithes, but yet he was unhappy and could not make ends meet, even on a school principal's salary. He decided to fast and pray, and the Holy Spirit told him to quit his job and go into farming. Many of you may ask, "Farming? Not me, I have status and perks as a school principal."

Nevertheless, the man followed the direction from the Lord. He quit his job and started to farm in his backyard. He later had money to buy more land in which to farm. To cut a long story short, there was a problem with many of the farms in the area, but the Lord sustained him. His farm was the only one flourishing, and through it he was the only farmer that was able to sustain the land. He was able to feed all the people in his district and in the surrounding districts. He became a millionaire just by farming. This farmer declared that if he had remained a principal, he would not have accomplished God's plan for his life, and neither would he be a millionaire! The farmer prayed and got God's plan for his life. Then he obeyed, did something about it, and the Lord led him to where He wanted him to be. Many people would have starved to death if it had not been for the crops the farmer produced.

You see, sometimes the Lord calls us for reasons we do not know or understand, but if His plan for us is to sweep the streets, that is what we have to do, because maybe in sweeping the streets, we will meet people who will accept Jesus Christ as their Lord and Saviour, thus increasing God's Kingdom. God has a plan for each and every one of us. Let us pray and ask Him to reveal His plans for us and ask Him how to accomplish that which God wants us to accomplish. And just think, when we have to account for our time on Earth to our Father, our Father will say, "Well done!"

17
You Are a Conqueror!

You may have heard the phrase "You are a conqueror" over and over again, but how many of you know what being a conqueror really means? The Concise Oxford Dictionary states that "conqueror" means *"a person who conquers."*[4] This tells me, first and foremost, that in order to be a conqueror, one has to have something to conquer. What do you have to conquer: fears, problems, addictions? Secondly, in order to be a conqueror, you have to have the right tools, strategies, and know-how in order to be victorious.

FEARS

Fear. Where does it come from? What or who makes you afraid? What are you afraid of? Some of us are afraid of the dark, some of us are afraid of our husbands, some of us are afraid of success,

---

[4] *The Concise Oxford Dictionary (8th Edition).* Oxford University Press, New York, 1990. p.243

and many of us are afraid to change. When I say change, I mean to change spiritually, mentally, and physically. Change is good.

In Psalm 27:1, the Bible tells us that *"the Lord is my light and my salvation; whom shall I fear? The Lord is the strength of my life; of whom shall I be afraid?"* This scripture tells me that once you know you have the Lord Jesus Christ on your side, you should not have any fear of anything or anyone.

2 Timothy 1:7 declares, *"For God hath not given us the spirit of fear; but of power, and of love, and of a sound mind."* This means that fear does not come from God, and if fear is not generated by God, then it comes from the devil.

Anything that comes from the devil must be rejected. When I first accepted Jesus as my Lord and Saviour, I remember my pastor saying, "satan has paw, but no claw." In other words, he was telling us that satan will try, but he will not get at us because Jesus will fight our battles for us. Therefore, we must not be afraid.

I remember when I went back to university after having my children. satan used to convince me that I could not drive on the highway to get to the university. I had such a terrible fear of driving on the highway, although at the time I had had my license for over fifteen years. The distance from where I lived to where the university was located should have taken me half an hour of driving, but because of my fear of the highway, I took the long route, which took me over an hour. This went on for a few years, until I finally prayed about it, and the Lord said to me, "I am with you. You have nothing to fear." From that moment, I got into my car, drove on the highway, and guess what? It was easy, and I got to classes in half the time it took me to drive the long route. I thanked God for removing that fear from me. It may have seemed a simple thing, but it was huge for me. My Father in Heaven took it away and gave me the victory.

Why are you afraid? If you know who is at your right hand side, there is no need to be afraid. You may say, "Sure Juliet, but you are not with me when I have to write an exam or when I have to face my boss and be condemned by him everyday." No, I am not with you, but you have someone at your side at all times who is far greater than I am, and that someone is Jesus Christ. Jesus will remove all fears from you. I guarantee that once you ask Him, He will take your fears away.

Problems

Problems? Who has them? Is there anyone out there who does not have a problem? If you do not, then you need to check yourself, because once you are living for the Lord Jesus Christ, satan will tempt you, he will test you, and problems in some shape or form will come.

What are some of the problems you are dealing with? Some of you may be struggling with your spouse, some may be struggling with rebellious children, some may be struggling with your finances, while others may be struggling with more personal problems. Whatever the situation, I want you to know that God is on your side. He is sitting on His throne, and He is still in control.

Some of our problems may be minute, some of our problems may be great, but whatever it is, put God first and you will be amazed to see how He will work out your situation for you. I have proven God over and over again. Before I accepted Jesus as my Lord and Saviour, I thought of committing suicide on many occasions. I was frustrated, I was angry, and I really did not know better, I just wanted to end it all, but God, in His own way, sent people at the right place and at the right time to talk to me. Luckily for me, they obeyed His voice and I am still alive today.

Why do you think you have problems? Is it brought on by you or others? How do you deal with your problems? Do you worry and stress yourself out, or do you pray? Some of us like to blame others for every little thing that goes wrong in our lives, and sometimes we are the ones who are causing all the problems in our lives.

When I say we, I mean you and me. For example, when I get a breakthrough in something I have been praying for, I sometimes tend to slack off my prayer time, and that is when more problems come. I cannot blame satan; I have to blame myself, because I gave satan the opportunity to come in. When you sit and watch television for hours, or you talk on the phone for hours, and you barely make time to read your Bible and pray, after all that television and gossiping, you do not have the energy to spend quality time with the Lord. That is when satan comes in and problems come again.

We cannot always blame ourselves for our problems. We can also blame our ancestors for certain recurring problems. Yes, our ancestors. So many of our ancestors who were not saved, and even some who were saved, went to the Obeah man, the palm reader, the soothsayer, and whatever else you call it in your country. This has caused tremendous problems for our generation.

You may say, "But that was them. It has nothing to do with me." Brothers and sisters, it has everything to do with us. Many people's parents and grandparents went to these types of people for help because they did not know better. Some of them did not know the Lord Jesus Christ as their Saviour. When people go to these places, they think that they are getting help, but it is just the opposite. On many occasions, people have to sacrifice something in order to have their deed performed. Unfortunately, the sacrifice made was the future of their children and grandchildren.

Let me explain. When a sacrifice is made, sometimes animals are killed, and sometimes humans are killed. Do not be afraid of what I am telling you, for the Lord wants you to know about these things. When blood is shed for a sacrifice, it means that whatever was asked to be done, whether it is to kill an enemy, to invoke demons into a person, or to commit murders, whatever it is, it has to take place.

Sometimes, people sacrifice their own flesh and blood in order to do evil to others. I heard of a woman who paid an Obeah man to "tie" her son to marry a lovely girl, but the sacrifice was that he would never have any children. People sacrifice their daughters! So many women cannot have children because of the sacrifices that were performed generations before.

Many people have problems with their health. Some of you, if you check yourself, will find that you are sick around the same time every year, with the same aches and pains. Although you have been healed of it already, it continues to come back. Some of you may have financial difficulties, and you are always in debt. Your pay comes in in one hand, and in days your money is gone. You do not know how or where you spent it. They call that "leaking hands" or "leaking pockets." These are signs that evil was done somewhere along the line and it is manifesting in your life.

I know of Christians who turn to the Obeah man or Obeah woman for help. They know the Lord as their Saviour, yet they do not wait on the Lord. They want the quick solution. They do not realize that by turning to the Obeah man or the palm reader, they are no longer serving God; they are now serving satan.

All of you reading this book, please pay attention. The *solution is Jesus Christ.* Only Jesus can heal us, deliver us, and set us free. For those of you who think that the quick fix is what you need, think again. There are many consequences you will suffer if you go to those places, consequences that may follow you, your children, your grandchildren, and great-grandchildren for generations to come. So think long and hard before you turn to these people. In the end, you will end up in Hell. The only true way out of problems is through salvation, through Jesus Christ. When Jesus solves your problems, it will be resolved perfectly and permanently.

Sometimes the Lord allows us to go through problems so that we can grow in Him. If we never experienced problems, how could we prove God? If we never go through the tough times, how can we see God's miracles and wonders? When you experience difficulties, do not be dismayed. Do not fret. Just put God in the middle of it and obey Him. Watch how the Lord will work it out.

You may say, "My God, where are you?" when for weeks, months, maybe even years, you are going through the same problems. Note one thing: God will not give you anything you cannot handle, and when you cannot handle it, He handles it for you. Our God is able to do wonders for you and me. He is the Omnipotent One, the Alpha and Omega, the beginning and the end, and as I mentioned previously, before you were born, He knew you. He knows what you will go through even before you go through it, so why fret? Just put your trust in Him. Allow God to work things out for you. You will never fail if you put your trust in Him!

ADDICTIONS

You all know the popular addictions like smoking, drinking, and doing drugs, all of which are bad for you, but these topics have been covered already so I will not cover them again. However, I would like to talk to you about food addictions. I know I will hear many of you screaming at me for saying that coffee drinking is an addiction. I would also like to discuss sex addictions, and addiction to the television and video games.

FOOD ADDICTION

Let me begin with the addiction to food. The Bible tells us, in Proverbs 23:1-3, "*When thou sittest to eat with a ruler, consider diligently what is before thee: And put a knife to thy throat, if thou be a man given to appetite. Be not desirous of his dainties: for they are deceitful meat.*" In Proverbs 18:20, it states, "*A man's belly shall be satisfied with the fruit of his mouth; and with the increase of his lips shall he be filled.*" Also in Proverbs 10:11, it states, "*The mouth of a righteous man is a well of life: but violence covereth the mouth of the wicked.*"

My understanding of these scriptures is that before we eat, we must check to see what we are eating. If we know it is not good for us, then put it aside and eat what we know is right for us. I also believe that once we pray before we eat, the Lord will direct us as to what to eat, how much to eat, and the Holy Spirit will give us the ability to avoid foods that are harmful to our well-being.

When we use food as a means of comfort, it could become an addiction. I used food as my comforter for years, and all it did to me was pack on the pounds. It left me feeling, empty, lonely, and depressed.

I liked sweets—anything with coconut or nuts in it were my favourite. I would not be hungry, yet I would buy cookies, muffins, and chocolates. Andy used to tell me that I was addicted to sweets and that I was a sugarholic. Of course, I used to tell him I was not, but deep down I knew I was.

For years, I battled with an addiction to sweets. I would go to dinners and parties only for the deserts, not so much to be in the company of friends… I really went for the deserts. While I was in the stage of my addiction to sweets, I knew what triggered me. If I was bored, if I was upset, if I was frustrated, or if I was told about my weight, I went to "pig out" on the sweets. How many of you are going through what I went through?

The moment I tried to exercise and eat right, that was when the cravings for the sweets would come on stronger than ever. Whenever Andy and I had a disagreement, I would go for the sweets, just to spite him, knowing fully well that I was doing it to my own body and not his.

So many of us see obese people and we ask ourselves, how could they eat pizza, or how could they eat another slice of cake after eating so much food? We may even make comments about their eating habits. Meanwhile, we do the same thing in private. Yet we judge them.

Because of our human nature, we are susceptible to all forms of addictions. I know of two ministers who struggle with addictions: one is addicted to drinking coffee and the other is addicted to drinking coke (the carbonated beverage). satan will attack anyone, from the average church member to the pastor. The addiction to food is a spiritual matter. You see, our body is the temple of the Holy Ghost; we are to keep it clean and healthy. This is why satan plants addictions in our heads. He will whisper to us, "You're bored, why not eat the last piece of cake in the fridge before anyone else can get to it?" Or he may say, "What is another cookie going to do to you? What is another cup of coffee or can of coke going to do? Nothing. Just have it, it will taste so good." Then, without thinking, we will get up and get the cookie, the cake, the coffee, the coke, or whatever else we are addicted to.

Some people may say that we do not have any self-control, and that we should learn to control ourselves. I am writing to tell you that self-control is not the issue. The real issue is knowing that it is satan who is controlling you. He is the one that whispers to you, "Pig out." If you know that when you are bored you tend to eat unhealthy foods, pray about it and then find something to do that will take your mind off the food: start reading, or go for a walk. Find something to occupy your time, and I guarantee you that the cravings for the food, the sweets, and the coffee will go away.

What is the solution? The solution to food addictions is prayer, perseverance, and patience. I once saw on a well-known television program that there was a woman who had a problem with food addictions. She did not pay any money to see a therapist, she simply prayed. She said, "Every time I feel the urge to eat junk food, I would ask the Holy Spirit to take away the cravings, and to help me." She said it worked and within a few months she had lost her unwanted weight and she was no longer addicted to food.

An addiction to food does not come on overnight, so be very patient in trying to rid yourself of this addiction. Examine yourself at all times. Ask yourself, "Am I really hungry? Didn't I just eat a half-hour ago? What is causing me to want to eat again? The most important tool in battling food addictions is asking the Holy Spirit to take total control of everything you put into your mouth. Believe me, it is the most powerful tool you will ever need in battling your addiction to food.

Sex Addiction

Sex is good when it is between a man and a woman who are married to each other. Sex is ordained by God. Sex is used to procreate, and therefore it is good. Sex is important in a married couple's relationship.

If someone is addicted to sex, it means that he or she wants to have sex everyday, many times a day, whether they're married or not. Sometimes such an individual will have sex with friends on a casual basis, other times he or she will have sex with a friend's spouse, and other times he or she will pay someone for sex, whether it is someone of the same sex or opposite sex.

If you are a sex addict, or know someone who is a sex addict, please know that this too is a spirit that is controlling you. Sex demons are causing you to want sex twenty-four hours a day, seven days a week. I remember, when I was growing up in Tobago, there was a young girl, in her teens, who went around looking for men to have sex with her on a daily basis. The people on the island used to say that "somebody put her so." In other words, evil was done to her and the result was that she had to have sex to survive, and if she did not, she would die.

Many people out there are addicted to sex. Please do not misunderstand me: sex is good, when it is in the context of marriage. According to God's principles, when you are married, if you choose to have sex three times a day, and both parties are in agreement, that is fine. You may say to me, "But there are some sex addicts who are married too. Is that all right?" I am saying that once one is married, and both husband and wife agree to having sex many times a day, then their actions are appropriate. In Hebrews 13:4, the Bible states, *"Marriage is honourable in all, and the bed undefiled: but whore-mongers and adulterers God will judge."*

I am concerned with those people who are going around from sex partner to sex partner. Such an individual needs spiritual deliverance. First and foremost, you must ask God to forgive you.

114

YOU ARE A CONQUEROR!

You must accept Jesus Christ as your Lord and Saviour. You must pray and ask God to deliver you from this deadly spirit.

If you do not get delivered from a sex demon, one of two things will take place. Firstly, you will continue having sex with everyone you meet. You will not have any meaningful relationship or marriage. Secondly, you will also be frustrated and angry, with no hope of living a purposeful life, which will eventually lead to your death. Yes, death. When I say death, I mean you can contract fatal diseases which have no cures.

Having a sex addiction can lead you to commit crimes. For example, if you cannot get a consenting adult to have sex with you, you may end up raping young girls or women, or you may get involved in pornography.

If you now realize that you have a sex addiction, please pray. Seek spiritual guidance from a Spirit-filled church. Ask the pastor to help pray for your complete deliverance from this addiction and seek professional help.

ADDICTION TO TELEVISION AND VIDEO GAMES

This one may seem simple to understand. When you are glued to the television and video games, this is an addiction. Many of us, both young and old, have this addiction. If I am not careful, I too can sit in front of the television and look at it all day. I always have to check myself.

What causes this addiction? Sometimes you just find yourself glued to the television and video games, and sometimes it just "takes you in." You do not know why you play those games. Some of you play the deadliest games, the bloodiest games, the goriest games, yet you do not understand the consequences of these games, or even the consequences of watching certain television shows.

THE SILENT DEATH

Many video games have subliminal messages in them. Many of these games cause people to do things that they would not normally do. Just recently, in Toronto, two teenaged boys were caught speeding on a residential street. One of the teenagers ended up crashing his parents' Mercedes Benz into a taxi and the taxi driver died instantaneously. At the scene of the crash, the police examined the teenagers and found a video game in one of the teenager's car. The police said that the teenagers were performing the same stunts they saw in the video game.

Watching television and playing video games may seem harmless, but note that the time you waste watching all that television and playing video games is time you could be spending studying God's word and praying. It is time you could be spending with your family. It is time you could be spending trying to better yourself educationally, spiritually, physically, and emotionally.

ENEMIES

Enemies, we all have them. Who are our enemies? What do they look like? How are they disguised? Many of you think that your enemies are the persons who you do not speak to anymore, or the people who did you wrong. I am telling you that your enemies are the people who are right next to you: your family, your in-laws, your friends, your co-workers, your colleagues, and your brothers and sisters in Christ who praise God with you on a Sunday.

My mother Marie always told Claudette and me, "It is not your enemies who will do you wrong, it is your friends. Your enemies cannot get to you, but your friends can get to you, so be careful of your friends." My mother was a very wise woman. In reviewing my life, I realized that she was one hundred percent true.

You Are a Conqueror!

Why do you have enemies? What makes them your enemies? We have enemies for the slightest reasons. For example, people hate us for simple reasons, such as we are blessed, or people are jealous of us because doors of opportunity are opened unto us instead of them.

Enemies are real. They may disguise themselves as your best friend, your helper, your spouse, your co-worker, or your brethren in Christ. No matter who your enemy is, how do you handle them? How you handle your enemies will determine your success over them.

When you handle your enemies with white gloves, it means that you know they are your enemy, yet you move carefully around them. You still talk to them, you still laugh with them, you may have them at the back of your mind at all times, but you still take things from them and try not to hurt their feelings.

My daughter Kristin was like that. She knew of a certain girl in her school who was so jealous of her. Kristin was the only friend this girl ever had in high school and in university, yet this so-called friend stabbed her in the back on many occasions. It was not until the Lord revealed certain things to Kristin and to me concerning this so-called friend that Kristin decided to change her attitude towards this girl. Kristin decided to take off the white gloves and let God direct her in this battle over her enemy.

Sometimes we need to fight our enemies with Holy Anger. Yes, Holy Anger. When I say Holy Anger, I mean, you should not do things to please them. Now is time for the Holy Spirit and the angels of the living God to fight for you. Do not be afraid to ask the Holy Spirit to fight for you. Your personal angel of the Living God is waiting for you to issue him the command to fight against your enemies. First of all, you have to ask the Holy Spirit to identify your enemies for you. Once your enemies are identified, the Holy Spirit will direct you as to how to deal with them. Once the Lord Jesus Christ is at your side, He will fight for you. The traps your enemies set for you, they themselves will fall into them.

Micah 7:5-6 states, *"Trust not in a friend, put ye not confidence in a guide: keep the doors of thy mouth from her that lieth in thy bosom. For the son dishonoureth the father, the daughter riseth up against her mother, the daughter in law against her mother in law; a man's enemies are the men of his own house."* This means that enemies will come from your own household, among your own family.

Once you are living for the Lord, you will always have enemies. Jesus said in Matthew 5:43-44, *"Ye have heard that it hath been said, Thou salt love they neighbour, and hate thine enemy. But I say unto you, Love your enemies, bless them that curse you, do good to them that hate you, and pray for them which despitefully use you, and persecute you."* In other words, forgive them and bless them.

This is not easy sometimes, but we have to do it. We have to know that it is not the physical person who is doing us the evil things; it is satan that is controlling them to hate us, to be jealous of us, and it is satan's plan to use our enemies to destroy us. I am not saying that you should allow them to walk over you. No, I am saying that once you identify that it is satan that is using your enemies against you, let God fight your battle for you.

The Bible says that vengeance belongs to God. Let the Lord deal with your situation. If you try to deal with it on your own, you will fail, so let the Lord have his way in your situation, and you will see how He will work out the situation. I have seen in my own life how the Lord dealt with my enemies. He had them under my feet at all times. They were like my footstool. They could not function when I was around them, praise the Lord!

I have touched on many things in this chapter. I want you to know that you are a Conqueror. In order to be a conqueror, you would have had to experience fear, problems, an addiction, and an enemy for you to conquer. Through the Blood of Jesus, we have the victory. The Blood of Jesus gives us the victory over our fears, our addictions, our problems, and our enemies. The Blood of Jesus gives us the victory in every area of our lives. By fasting, praying, waiting on God, having patience, and fighting the good fight, you will have the victory.

A pastor once said, "Tie your knot and hang on. Your answer is around the corner." In other words, when you have a problem, an addiction, a fear, or an enemy, tie a knot and hang on, pray and God will answer you. He will fight for you. If you let go of the knot, you will miss God's answer, so tie that knot and hang on tight. You are a Conqueror because Jesus Christ never fails. He is with you at all times. All you have to do is call on Him. Today, know that you are a Conqueror because Jesus is at your right hand side. If He never fails and you are living for Him, it means that you too will never fail. You are a Conqueror!

18

Your Destiny Is Sure Once You Are Living for Jesus

On many occasions throughout this book, I have mentioned the word destiny, but what does destiny really mean? According to the Concise Oxford Dictionary, "destiny" means *"the predetermined course of events; fate; regarded as a power; what is destined to happen to a particular person."*[5]

Have you ever asked yourself what is your destiny? I know I have. I asked myself why was I born and for what purpose was I put on this Earth. Maybe you too have asked these same questions.

---

[5] *The Concise Oxford Dictionary (8th Edition).* Oxford University Press, New York, 1990. p.317

As the dictionary states, destiny is a predetermined course of events. It is something that is inevitably going to happen to a person. What do you think your destiny has in store for you? While many of us thought that we would become a famous movie star, a brilliant doctor, or a lawyer, others felt that they would simply be ordinary people, doing ordinary jobs. Yet still others aspire to become parents and grandparents.

Whatever you think you ought to do, think again, because sometimes what you think you want to do is totally opposite from what God intends for you to do here on Earth.

I am writing to tell you that you do not have to settle for any old life, or any old job. Once you accept Jesus Christ as your Lord and Saviour, your destiny is sure. You know that you will end up in Heaven. If you have not accepted Jesus Christ as your Lord and Saviour, and you are not living for Jesus, it means you are living for satan, and you will be destined for Hell. We must focus on where we will end up after we die.

Some people believe that they should live as they please and that it does not matter to them where their soul ends up. Others believe that once they give to the poor and live a good life, they will make it into Heaven. Some people do not care where they end up after they die. If only these people knew how serious life really is. You see, we are just passing through this life here on Earth; our final destination is where our soul will reside for eternity, and it is important. Whether we're destined for Heaven or Hell should matter to each and every one of us.

Recently, Andy's cousin and her friend were visiting with us from the United States. While they were visiting with us, I discovered that the friend, whom I will call Bev, did not believe in Jesus Christ. She believed that things simply happened without the control of a supreme being. Well, you should know me by

121

now. My motto in my home is that I must tell anyone who visits my home about Jesus.

They were in my home for four days, so I knew I did not have much time to share my belief. I prayed about it, and the Lord had it that I was in bed with pain for two out of the four days. One day, Andy took his cousin out to shop while Bev remained at home with me. As I lay on my bed, we started to talk about a variety of issues which eventually led to a discussion about Jesus Christ. To cut a long story short, I was able to witness to her. I told her about curses, I told her about God's love for us and His blessings, and we discussed Heaven and Hell. She did not accept Jesus Christ as her Lord and Saviour there, but the day she was leaving she asked me to pray for their safe return home. I prayed and I thanked God that the seed was sown in her. It is up to God, in His time, to water that seed and to bring it to fruition.

We must not be afraid or ashamed to tell friends and relatives about Jesus, because if we do not witness to them, who will? How will they know the truth? How will they know the consequences of not living for Jesus? How will they make it into Heaven if they do not know about Jesus?

Many of us are afraid or ashamed to witness for Jesus. We are afraid of what our friends may say about us, but who cares what they say? We will not have to answer to them when we die. However, we will have to answer to God. What we should be ashamed of is if we are given the opportunity to witness and we do not. We should be very afraid to meet God on that judgment day if we wasted our time and if we felt embarrassed to witness to others.

What are the things that God desires of us? God desires a pure heart, a contrite spirit, love for Him and others, and most importantly, acceptance of Jesus Christ as our Lord and Saviour and our commitment to Him. Once we know we are doing these things, our destiny will be sure in Christ Jesus.

If you are not heeding God's words, if you are not living for Him, if you choose to live any way you want and do anything to please yourself and others, it means you are not heeding God's words or His plans for your life, and this will result in death and everlasting damnation.

My Aunt Sislyn was recently diagnosed with cancer. Between her diagnosis and her death was approximately eight weeks. Thank God my aunt accepted Jesus as her Lord and Saviour and she lived a Christian life. When I found out about her diagnosis, I called her. The first thing she said to me was that she was ready to meet her Maker. She said that she would not go through the chemotherapy because she was ready, ready to go home.

I believe that she knew, although she did not tell me, her end was near and she did not want to go through the treatments. She was anxious to go home to meet her Lord, she was happy to know that her end was near, and when she died in her sleep, I knew that she made it into Heaven.

The beauty of it all is that she knew where her destiny was when she passed from this life. She was one hundred percent sure that she would be home with the Lord. She was happy, she was excited, and that is how we ought to be—happy and excited to be with our Lord when our time comes. Nevertheless, we can only be excited and happy to go if we know where our destiny will be taking us.

Is your destiny with the Lord, in Heaven? Or is your destiny with satan, in Hell? The choice is yours. Just remember: your destiny is sure if you have accepted Jesus Christ as your Lord and Saviour and if you are living for Him. Make your choice, but do not delay, because tomorrow may be too late.

19
Give Glory to God That You Are Born Again

If you have finally given your heart to the Lord and you have accepted Jesus Christ as your Lord and Saviour, praise be to God! Give God the glory that you are born again! What do you do next? The first thing you should do, if you have not done so already, is to find a spirit-filled church, a place where they preach about Jesus and the Holy Spirit. After you have joined a spirit-filled church, pray and ask God for direction. Be a part of the church. Do not only attend on Sundays, but instead be an active member. Either join the youth department, the women's ministry, or the men's ministry. Get involved. This will help you to grow in the Lord.

Just think about where the Lord brought you from and where you are going in the Lord. Reflect and give God the praise. Always give God the praise, the honour, and the glory due to His name. I remember when the seed of salvation was sown in me. It was while I was on vacation in Tobago, twenty-four years ago.

I did not know what happened. Claudette invited me to her home for a prayer meeting. When I got there, it was only the two of us at the meeting. She sang some songs, she prayed, and that was it. After I left her home and came back to Canada, I realized that I somehow wanted to know more about God. I wanted to pray and read my Bible and I just felt like something was missing. I told the Lord that if this was Him, let me find a spirit-filled church to attend. Lo and behold, within a few days, a Pentecostal minister and his wife came knocking on my apartment door. They invited me to come to their church, and it was at this church that I accepted Jesus as my Lord and Saviour.

It can be as simple as that. You may go to a crusade or hear someone preach on television or on the radio, or it can be a friend who is witnessing to you. Whoever it is you are hearing about God from, just note that it is the Holy Spirit quickening you to come to the Lord Jesus Christ. You may say, "Oh, it is only in my head." Yes, it is in your head, but it is the Holy Spirit who has put it there to invite you to accept Jesus as your Lord and Saviour.

Some people find it so difficult to accept and live for Jesus. Some people give all kinds of excuses. I remember some of my excuses. The main reason for me was that I could not wear my pants, my jewellery, and my makeup. I know it may sound stupid, but in those days, when my sister gave her heart to the Lord, one was not permitted to wear jewellery, makeup, or pants. It was against the church's rules. At that time, I did not want to give up those things, so I rebelled and turned away from Christ. I continued in my Catholic church, and continued committing sin.

I am grateful that I finally made the decision to commit my life to Jesus Christ. Otherwise, I don't know where I would have ended up, maybe dead and in Hell. I know the life that I had and

I know the path I was following, and I would not have made it to see today.

Many generational curses were put upon me which were to ultimately result in my death. Praise be to God that my Lord and Saviour Jesus Christ had other plans for my life, and by me accepting Jesus into my life, my destiny has changed. My life is rewarding and I will live to fulfill God's plans for my life.

What are some of you waiting on? In many churches today, you are allowed to wear pants, jewellery, and makeup, so that should not be your excuse like it was mine. In many churches today, there are various groups for all ages, so you can meet and be with people your own age. In many churches, the anointing of God is so strong that prophecies are given, healings take place, deliverance takes place, and we can see for ourselves the power of God. We no longer have to hear from someone in a faraway land. Right here in Toronto, miracles are taking place on a daily basis.

I have seen with my own eyes the lame walk and deliverance from evil and death. I have seen it with my own eyes, so what is your excuse? You may say to me that you are not ready. However, my response to you is, what are you waiting on? When will you be ready? Are you waiting for God to come back to Earth, because by then it will be too late! I say to you, you do not know the time nor the hour that our Lord Jesus Christ will return. The Bible tells us in Revelation 22:12, that Jesus is coming back quickly. Friends, He is coming back soon, so you may not have tomorrow to give your heart to the Lord. Now might be your only time, your only chance to surrender your life to Him.

By now, you must be tired of reading about accepting Jesus as your Lord and Saviour, but I am not going to stop writing about it, because it is serious; we are talking about your eternal life. We are talking about the place where you will spend your eternity.

The Bible tells us that before Jesus comes back to Earth, everyone will have an opportunity to hear about Him. This might be your last chance to hear about Jesus, so do not delay, accept Him as your Lord and Saviour.

In a previous chapter, I mentioned an eighth grade student who did not believe in God. This same young man recently told me that his grandmother, who lives in Russia, accepted Jesus as her Lord and Saviour. Praise be to God! Look at what the Lord is doing. He is reaching people all over the world. Allow Him to reach you today.

REASONS WHY YOU SHOULD ACCEPT
JESUS CHRIST AS YOUR LORD AND SAVIOUR

1. Jesus died for you and for me. He sacrificed His life for us. It is because of Him that we have everlasting life.

2. When you accept Jesus as your Lord and Saviour, you are given power to defeat satan, his agents, and his plans for your life. satan is defeated and will always be defeated, but when you have Jesus in your heart and you are living for Him, you are given power to dethrone satan, his angels, his agents, and all their plans for your life.

3. You will have victory in every area of your life. Sometimes things may look bleak and hopeless, but if you put your trust in Jesus and you put Him first, the Lord will direct your path as to where you ought to be and the things you have to do in order to experience victory in your life.

4. If you are not living for Jesus, it means that you are living for the devil. When you live for the devil, you will be controlled by him and you will do things for him, which will lead you to destruction, failure, and death. In the end,

you will have no peace, no joy, no happiness, and the end result will be Hell, where you will spend eternity.

These are just some of the reasons why you should accept Jesus Christ as your Lord and Saviour. I promise that if you do this today, you will never regret it. You will see the glory of God upon you and experience real joy, peace, and happiness. You will always have Jesus at your side to fight your battles and I guarantee that you will win them. Most importantly, if you give your life to Jesus, He will direct you, guide you, love you, and He will never leave you. Victory will always be yours and, in the end, you will spend eternity with Him in Heaven, which is the ultimate promise!

20
For Men Only: Ways to Treat a Woman

W hy did my Father in Heaven ask me to write this chapter? I cannot say, but it must be important, otherwise He would not have asked me to write it. Men, please do not think that I am attacking you. No, there is a need for men to know exactly how to treat a woman.

Some men treat women the way they treat their mothers. Other men treat women the way they treat their pets. Still others treat women as if they are the most beautiful and most important being on this planet. Whichever category you fall into, sit back and note the ways that God wants you to treat a woman. If you are a spirit-filled man that is obedient to Christ, it will make the task easier.

I will be discussing two categories. The first list will be referring to how a man must treat a woman and the second list will be referring to how a man must treat his wife.

The Following List Refers to
How a Man Must Treat a Woman

Know that a woman, whether she is your mother, sister, aunt, cousin, wife, colleague, or friend, needs to be respected, loved, and appreciated.

1. Women need to be listened to, not talked down to.
2. Do not assume that women must do everything. There are some things women cannot do.
3. Do not go back on your word. It makes you look untrustworthy.
4. Women like to feel as if they have contributed to the household, not only financially, but also spiritually and emotionally.
5. Don't be angry for every little thing.
6. When you know your woman has really tried to do something right, do not show your disappointment in her when it comes out wrong. Encourage her, direct her, and comfort her.
7. Control your temper at all times. This just makes you look as if you do not have any self-control.
8. Spend quality time with God. He will direct your relationship, your decisions, and your destiny.
9. Never lead a woman into thinking you will marry her. If you don't marry her, this pain never dies.
10. Encourage your woman to strive for her best, to do her best.

11. Control your jealousy. Women do not like jealous men.
12. Never backbite or backstab a woman. You will live to regret it.
13. Handle your woman with tender care.
14. Never allow your friends or family to control your relationship.
15. If you have a best friend, whether male or female, note that your girlfriend comes first.
16. Do not be afraid to say, "I'm sorry." Saying I'm sorry and asking for forgiveness will go a long way in your relationship.
17. Get rid of your pride. Pride will kill you.
18. Be gentle, be kind, and be loving, no matter the circumstances.
19. Work hard at your relationship. It will pay off in the end.
20. Do not take your woman for granted. She may slip away from you without you knowing it.
21. Have a positive attitude.
22. Do not procrastinate, but do things right away. Tomorrow may be too late.
23. Live a simple but honest life. Women do not like when things are complicated.
24. Strive for the top. Aim high.
25. Elevate your standard of living. Do not stay in the same rut all the time.
26. Spend quality time with your woman.
27. Share your dreams, aspirations, and wealth with her.
28. Discuss your fears with her.
29. Show that you are human. Do not pretend that everything is always okay.
30. Be proud of her accomplishments and show it.

31. Do not harp on the past, such as past boyfriends or past failures.
32. Be sympathetic.
33. Be a man, a good man, one who she will be proud to call her husband.
34. Be gentle.
35. Be understanding.
36. Do not ask too many questions, especially when she does not want to talk.
37. Set realistic goals.
38. Do not settle for mediocrity. Aim for greatness.
39. Share everything with her, even if you think she will be angry with you.
40. Be Christ-like. Think before you take action.
41. Be faithful at all times.
42. Be practical.
43. Feel free to cry in front of your woman. It shows that you are human.
44. Do not try to justify your wrongdoings.
45. Get rid of your doubts about marrying her. By doubting, you are giving satan the victory.
46. Study God's Word together.
47. It is still nice to open doors for her, pull out her chair, and make her feel like a queen.
48. Prophecy good things into your woman's life. Your words are powerful and they can either bring blessings or curses.
49. Treat your woman the way you want to be treated.
50. Love your woman wholeheartedly and unconditionally. Love her no matter what she looks like. Simply, love her.

FOR MEN ONLY: WAYS TO TREAT A WOMAN

THE FOLLOWING LIST REFERS TO HOW A MAN MUST TREAT HIS WIFE

1. Women do not like you making passes at other women in front of their faces.

2. Women like their men to be in church with them, not just sending the children to church. Men need to be the spiritual leader in the home as well as the head of the home.

3. A man needs to be sensitive to the emotional needs of his wife. Know when she is drained, when she needs consoling, and when to back off.

4. Pray, play, and purchase together. This reduces stress in a marriage.

5. Show your appreciation for the little things she does. Buy her flowers now and then. Surprise her with a gift, or dinner, or just a night away from her regular routine.

6. Contribute to the running of the household financially, physically, spiritually, mentally, and most of all, help with the chores and the rearing of your children.

7. Treat your wife the way you would treat your mother, if not better.

8. Put your wife on a pedestal and keep her there.

Many of the points in the first list can be applied to the second, as well.

Love conquers all things. When you show love to your woman or wife, when you treat her with respect, with kindness and with dignity, you in turn will be respected. Women look not only on the outside, but also on the inside of a man. Women observe men around children. They observe how men handle different situations, so if you do things underhandedly or with little regard for the people around you, she will note this and think that you are not worthy to be with her.

I trust that this chapter has accomplished what the Lord wants it to accomplish in your life. Just remember: women like to be treated equally and fairly. Do not judge them for the things they cannot do. Look at them from the inside out. Sometimes you have to take the time, quality time, to really know your woman or wife. Make her feel wanted, appreciated, and loved. At the end of the day, your relationship with her is what really matters, so give her your best and she, in turn, will give you her best.

21
The Traps of the Enemy

I n this chapter, I will focus on the various traps the enemy has for us, traps that we do not know exist, traps which lead us to our deaths.

TRAP 1: FRIENDS

Let us focus on your friends. How many of you have friends who at the beginning of your friendship would bend over backwards for you? They helped you out in different situations, and they were really there for you. Suddenly, things changed between you two. For no reason at all, your friends have stopped calling you, he or she has stopped spending time with you, and the whole relationship has altered, yet you do not know the cause of this change.

I have a friend who talked to me on the phone several times a week for many years. I witnessed to her. I prayed for her and with her. I was there when she found out her husband was having an affair and I held her hand and walked her through this difficult time. She accepted Jesus Christ at my home and I was the one who fasted and prayed with her. Do not get me wrong: I am not bragging, nor do I want a ribbon for bringing her to the Lord. I am just demonstrating how close we were and the things we went through together.

When I became ill and had to stop working, I realized that she changed towards me. She stopped calling me as often, she made new friends at her church, and she started keeping things from me. Over the years, our friendship has come down to me calling her once in a while, and if I did not call her, she would not call me. I did not know why she changed towards me, but I later realized that the spirit of jealousy had entered into her. I also realized that she did not need me anymore, because for one, I was not in the workforce anymore, and two, I was not able to go on trips with her and do the things we used to do.

I learned that although she attends church regularly, she and her new friends drink, something I knew she had given up when she became a Christian. You see, satan sets traps for us sometimes. This is a trap he set for my friend and she fell right into it. She became a Christian, the Lord helped her through many situations in her marriage, with her relatives, and on her job, and yet somehow she allowed satan to come back into her life. This is unfortunate.

Today, I see her grabbing at everything. Now she wants everything that others have, and her life has changed. She is not the same person she used to be. She lies, she pretends, and she has become covetous. satan set his trap for her, she fell into it, and now she is going down a path of destruction, a road that, if she does not go back to the Lord, will only lead her to more problems.

I remember what my mother always said: "Friends will take you, but they will not bring you back, so choose them wisely." In other words, be careful who you choose as your friend. Friends will come and friends will go, but it is the friend that will stick with you through thick and thin, the one who is walking on the same path as you, who will make it in the end.

satan will use your friends to divert you from where God wants you to be. He uses your friends to distract you, to dissuade you, and to discourage you from doing the things you know you should be doing—the right things.

TRAP 2: MONEY

Money, they say, is the root of all evil. Having money as your God is another trap that you could fall into which will make you lose your salvation, your calling, and your destiny with Christ. Again, I do not want you to think that I am saying that money is not good. Not at all. Money is good, being rich is great, and the Lord wants us to have money. What I am referring to is making money the number one focus of your life. I know of many young people who ran after the money in different companies, only to find themselves in trouble. I am talking about Christian men and women who did not pray and ask God for direction. They just went ahead and took positions because of the big paycheque and some of them ended up on drugs, some of them ended up losing their Christianity, and some others ended up dead.

Some people steal and commit sin to get money. Money is good, but if you are running after the mighty dollar and forget God and His plans for your life, you will miss the mark.

Many of you are accustomed to making ends meet with what you have. Sometimes people allow money and the lure of it to change their lifestyle, which will in turn change their destiny. Be careful of this trap. Always pray about it, ask God if that new job or big promotion is where He wants you to be. If He answers yes, then go for it. If He says no, then leave it alone. I have known people who went after the Mighty Dollar, only to be stressed, end up with heart attacks, or even die. Beware of this deathly trap of the enemy.

TRAP 3: THE OPPOSITE SEX

If you are male, be careful of females; if you are female, be careful of males. When a man says to a woman, "I love you; prove that you love me," be careful. Young men are famous for telling young girls, "I love you, and if you love me, have sex with me." This is a trap. I have come across many girls who fell for this trap and they ended up pregnant, left alone, disgraced, and disheartened. This trap has been around for a long, long time. Guys used that line on me in high school. Another line they used was, "Oh Juliet, Juliet, here is your Romeo."

Many girls end up having to leave school because of unwanted pregnancy. They are put out of their homes and some even end up on the streets because they do not have an education or a decent-paying job, so they end up as prostitutes. Other girls and women have abortions, which scars them mentally, physically, and emotionally for life. Some girls and their children end up on welfare, and the cycle continues.

satan uses women also to divert men from their divine destiny. Some women are used to corrupt men. Some women are used to take men away from their wives and families. Some women are used to sow seeds of confusion into men's lives. Some women are used to rob men of their money, their time, their walk with Christ, and their calling on this earth.

Men, beware of the wolf in sheep's clothing. Some women use their nice clothes and their perfumes to lure men. Some women use evil to get men for themselves. In Tobago, they called this "left hand dumpling." If someone said to you that you ate a "left hand dumpling," it meant that the woman had trapped you into marrying her by feeding you evil food. In other words, she put a potion in your food for you to marry her.

I remember a guy I knew when I was eighteen—I'll call him John. John had all the girls falling all over him. He was cute, but at the time I had a boyfriend, so I was not interested in him. John slept with every girl in sight. After a while, I found myself being attracted to him and it was as if I had to find ways to be around him. Eventually, I went out with him behind my boyfriend's back.

I found it strange when I was around him. It was as if he was controlling me. I wanted to be around him all the time and my boyfriend and I started having fights for no reason. I also started losing interest in my boyfriend. That's when a friend of my mom's had a dream about John and me. In the dream, she saw where John used to spray himself with certain herbs, and it was these herbs that were drawing me to him. He used this so-called "perfume" to get girls to go to bed with him. Thank God that the Lord protected me and I was able to escape this trap the enemy set for me.

This trap goes both ways. Men use evil to get women, and women use evil to get men. Whichever way it goes, it is a trap that both men and women have to be aware of. satan uses this trap to disgrace men and women, to destroy them, and to divert them from where God wants them to be.

The Silent Death

Trap 4: Debt

I know we spoke about money as being the number two trap, but in that case I was addressing the *lure* of money. This trap is dealing with debt. So many of us want, want, want! When we want everything, we tend to go into debt to get them. Andy, my husband, always says, "It is not what you want; it is what you need." He is right!

Some of us want things that we see our friends and family have: a new car, a bigger house, or the top of the line stereo, for example. But do we really need these things? I live in a house right now that has two kitchens. Do I need that? No, we only use one kitchen and the other one is used when we have guests, which is not very often, so why do we need this house with two kitchens?

Some of us must have the best name brand clothes. Again, do not misunderstand me: if you can afford it, go for it. However, if you cannot afford it, you will only be creating unnecessary debt.

When you are greedy and envious of others, you are led into debt. If you have to have whatever your friends have, this leads to debt! Debt leads to more debt, which in turn leads to anger, frustration, illness, suicide, and the breakup of homes.

If you really need something but cannot afford it, save for it, plan for it, and then get it when you have the money. Do not just max your credit cards out. Do not continue to borrow from family and friends when you know that you will not be able to pay them back. This will cause friction in families, breakup of friendships, and in the end, terrible heartache. Beware of trap number four, the trap of debt. When you fall into this trap, sometimes it is very difficult to come out of it. Sometimes, it even leads to your death.

The Traps of the Enemy
Trap 5: Spiritual

Have you ever noticed that you can sit and watch television for hours and feel fine, but as soon as you pick up your Bible to read, or decide to pray to God, you start to yawn and feel tired? This is the enemy's trap. satan does not want you spending time with God.

Be very careful. Sometimes you are eager to go on a fast, and that is the time when you will feel so hungry that you could eat everything in sight. In the past, you were on fire for the Lord, witnessing to everyone you met, yet today, you are afraid to witness. You are embarrassed to approach people and to let them know that you are living for the Almighty God.

Some people once took their Bibles and tracts on the train with them in order to minister to and witness to others. You no longer do that anymore. Instead, you have a romance novel or a gossip newspaper in your hand. Beware! These are the areas that satan uses to rob you spiritually. You see, when you are spiritually dead, how will you know which strategies satan uses against you, and how will you be able to defeat him?

When you do not pray, how will you be able to fight against those who fight against you? How will you know what God's plans are for your life? How will you be able to live for Jesus? How will you be a champion in God's Kingdom? This is a major trap that satan uses for the people of God, because without prayer and reading God's Words to fortify yourself daily in Christ, it will be easy for satan to control you. It will be easy for him to manipulate and destroy you, so be aware of this trap. Remember, when you are spiritually dead in Christ, you might as well be physically dead, because it is in the spiritual realm that many decisions about your life take place.

TRAP 6: CONTROLLING WHAT YOU LISTEN TO

Many people hear voices. On some occasions, it is the Lord's voice... but in other times, it is the voice of the devil himself. It is very important to pay attention to what you listen to. Many of the youth today listen to non-Christian songs. These songs give you subliminal messages. The enemy uses the upbeat music to lure you, then the lyrics tell you things that are not of God. Be aware and be careful!

satan speaks to people. I remember when Gregory was learning to swim at age six. Andy and I had put Kristin and Gregory in the water since they were six months old, so I knew that they were not afraid of being in a pool. At six years old, Gregory was in a class that first taught him how to dive off the diving board. Although Gregory was not afraid of the water, he was the only student in the class who would get to the tip of the diving board and refuse to dive into the water.

Greg would get to the tip of the board, look into the water, then turn back and end up crying. I found this to be strange, so one day I asked him why he did not want to jump off the diving board. He said, "Mom, every time I go up on the diving board, I hear a voice telling me that I cannot do it, and that if I dive, it will kill me." Remember, Greg was only six.

Since Greg was not a child who lied, I did not play around with what he told me. I told him that there was nothing to be afraid of, and that it was satan telling him those lies. I told him that I would pray for him, and that the Lord Jesus Christ would help him.

The next day when he went for his lesson, the Holy Spirit quickened me to go down to the pool and pray over the water. I prayed over Greg. I also prayed over the water in the pool and I commanded satan to flee and I told him that he was defeated. Praise be to God, on that same day, Greg did not hear any more voices. He climbed up to the diving board and dove into the pool. From that day on, he was able to dive into the pool without any fear, and he proved that God was in control and that he had the victory over satan.

At sixteen, Greg became a lifeguard and swim instructor. On his first day on the job, I reminded him of his experience when he was six, and I told him to use that experience to teach his students.

You see what satan tried to do to Greg? He tried to put fear in him. He tried to prevent him from accomplishing his goals, but he could not. The Lord Jesus Christ took away that fear and prevented satan from whispering in Greg's ears, and today Greg is fulfilling God's plans for him to be a swim instructor and lifeguard. Praise be to God!

Be careful with what you listen to, what you talk about, and what you watch. These are the traps that satan uses to destroy your life, your destiny, and your walk with Christ. I hope that now you are aware of some of the traps that the enemy uses to entangle you, to destroy you, and to divert you from your divine destiny. Remember: by reading God's word daily, by spending quality time with God, by praying and by waiting on the Lord for His direction, you will succeed in staying away from the traps of the enemy.

22

The Way Out

Some people lean on their own understanding, while others depend on the Obeah man, the soothsayer, or the fortune teller to direct them with what to do, when to do things, and how to do things. I am here to tell you that the only way out of satan's clutches, satan's lies, satan's roadmap for you, is through the Lord Jesus Christ.

I cannot emphasize this enough. Our Father in Heaven has a divine plan and purpose for your life. satan tries his best to disrupt God's plans for you. At all cost, satan tries to defeat you, and to lead you away from your divine destiny. The only way out is for you to accept Jesus Christ as your Lord and Saviour and to live wholeheartedly for the Lord.

When you accept Jesus Christ as your Lord and Saviour, your name will be written down in the Book of Life. When you accept Jesus Christ as your Lord and Saviour, you will be covered under the Blood of Jesus. Jesus Christ shed His Blood for you and me. Jesus Christ sacrificed it all on the cross of Calvary so that we, you and me, can have the victory.

The only way out of sickness, trials, tribulations, poverty, debt, problems, and death is through Jesus Christ. As I mentioned above, many people visit the Obeah man, the soothsayer, and the fortune teller. These people may tell you that they are of God, but they are *not* of God. They may perform their evil so that, for a time, you will get some results. I am telling you that these people are of the devil.

If you are dealing with Obeah, or using witchcraft to get what you want in life, stop it. It is a sin. These things are not permanent. If you deal in the occult to achieve greatness, a husband, or a wife, these things do not last. By involving yourself in witchcraft, you are making a pact with satan. Many people who have made this pact with satan have not lived to see their evil come to pass. Some people use evil to get ahead in life, while others use evil to put other people down in life. These people usually end up unhappy, frustrated, and some even die because of it.

They think that by doing evil, no one will find out. The non-Christians do not know what is wrong with them; they just think that the things that are going on in their lives are normal. The Christian ones, especially those that are really living for the Lord, always know. Greater yet, Jesus Christ knows what you are doing. Our Father in Heaven sees it all. The eternal place for people who perform evil, and those who participate in it, is in the fires of Hell. In Psalms 34:12-17, it says: "*What man is he that desireth life, and loveth many days, that he may see good? Keep thy tongue from evil, and thy lips from speaking guile. Depart from evil, and do good; seek peace, and pursue it. The eyes of the Lord are upon the righteous, and his ears are open unto their cry. The face of the Lord is against them that do evil, to cut off the remembrance of them from the earth. The righteous cry, and the Lord heareth, and delivereth them out of all their troubles."*

In other words, the Lord is telling us that we should stay away from evil, and that we must always strive to do good. He is also saying that God's eyes are upon those that do good, and He hears our cries. The Lord is against those that do evil, and he will cut off the remembrance of them from the earth. The Lord also said that when the righteous cry, He will hear our cries and deliver us out of *all* our troubles.

So those of you who know people who are dealing with the devil in any way, shape, or form, tell them that it is time to stop it. Tell them that it is time to repent, ask God to forgive them, accept Jesus as their Lord and Saviour, and turn a new leaf for Jesus. If they do not stop what they are doing, they will be doomed for eternity.

Some people may see suicide as their way out of situations and problems. Suicide is not the answer. Suicide is a spirit that is controlled by satan. I am speaking from experience. Many years ago, I was a new Christian and I was going through a rough time. No one knew, not even Andy. Kristin and Gregory were very young, and I was struggling with some issues.

satan told me that the only way out was to commit suicide. I remember being on the busiest highway one day, and I was thinking of crashing my car into the guardrail. The only thing that stopped me was when I remembered that both my kids were in the car with me.

There was another time when I thought of committing suicide. It was early in the morning and I could not sleep. I was tormented, and I remember sitting by the window looking up at the stars, and all that was going through my mind was how to end it all. satan told me that this was the only way out. He told me that I should end it all right then and there.

Praise be to God, the Lord knew what I was going through. It was at that very moment that my sister Claudette called me on the phone. This had nothing to do with twin intuition; this was the Holy Spirit that quickened her to call me. We spoke on the phone, and I cried like a baby. She had not known that I was contemplating suicide, so all she said was, "Jesus loves you, and He will see you through." After I hung up the phone, I began to pray. Somehow I knew that she was praying for me too, and that spirit of suicide was gone.

To this day, I never forgot what the Lord did for me. I know what it is like to feel frustrated, to feel like there is no end to what you are going through. This is what that old devil wants you to think, that there is no end to your problems and that there is no one to help you. I am here to tell you that satan is a liar. I am here to tell you that the Lord Jesus Christ is your way out. He is your answer to every stubborn situation. Jesus is the answer to your never-ending problems. Jesus is the answer to the abuse, the hardship, the poverty, the sickness, the humiliation, the debt, and to every thing that satan is throwing at you. *Jesus Christ is the answer, Jesus Christ is the way out!*

Jesus wants you to trust Him when you cannot see Him. Trust Him when there is no food on your table, when you do not know where your next rent cheque is coming from. Just trust Him. Trust Him when your husband cheats on you. Trust Him when your children go astray. Trust God when all else fails, because *Jesus Christ never fails!*

Trust God in every situation. When your family and friends give up on you, Jesus Christ will not give up on you. When you feel alone and that no one cares, Jesus cares for you. Our Father in Heaven wants you to live a rewarding life, a life of victory, a life of peace, love, joy, happiness, and prosperity—a life that will allow you to make it into Heaven with Him.

In order to end up in Heaven, you must first give Jesus a chance. Accept Jesus into your heart, live for Him, depend on Christ, and when trials come your way, you will have the victory. It may not be in our time, when we want things done, but in God's time. We will live to see how the Lord will work things out for us. Just look at me, satan wanted me to commit suicide years ago. If I had done that, where would I have been today? I would have been in Hell. If I had committed suicide, I would not have been able to accomplish what God put me here to accomplish, which is writing this book. I would have failed God.

Brothers and sisters in Christ, friends, all of you who are reading this book, please take me seriously. The only way out is through Jesus Christ. Others may tell you otherwise. Many may tell you to try different things, like evil—but that is not the answer. Jesus Christ is the only answer. Our Father in Heaven is the one who made you. He knows you inside and out. Our Father in Heaven sent His only begotten son, Jesus, to experience hardship, ridicule, and temptation for us. Jesus died for you and me, and it is through His death that our sins are forgiven and that we may have everlasting life. Jesus died for us so that we may have eternal life with Him. In order to have that eternal life, we must accept Him, love Him, and live for Him, so that one day we will be worthy to be with Him forever.

I remember when my mom Marie died eighteen years ago. My brother-in-law, Norman, sang a song at her funeral. I don't remember the name of the song, but the words went like this, "Where will you be a million years from now? Will you be happy? Will you be free?"

This song made me think of where I will end up after I die. This song comforted me because I knew that my mom made it into Heaven. How did I know? I know because she gave her heart to the Lord, accepting Jesus as her Lord and Saviour. She accepted Jesus only a few years before she died, but praise God, she did it! I want you to know, too, that no matter what time you are called home, if you accept Jesus Christ as your Lord and Saviour, and if you live for Him, you will be with Jesus for all eternity. I know that in the end, it will all be worth it.

My pastor, Evans Barning, preached his Good Friday service and his message was entitled, "Coming out of Darkness." In his message, he said that it was time for us to come out of our negativity. It was time for us to come out of the things that people say about us. He means that people constantly tell us what we can and cannot do. For example, your friends may tell you that you are stupid and that you will not amount to much. Others may say things like, "Who do you think you are? You will never get a job like that!"

Do not allow your family, friends, colleagues, or anyone else to tell you that you cannot accomplish your goals, your dreams, and your ambitions. No, that is a lie from satan himself. We are so programmed to always hear the word "No," that it is in our subconscious. Whenever we try to do something, we hear that voice telling us that we cannot. It is like when I wanted to go back to complete my university degree. For fourteen years, the devil told me I couldn't, but guess what? After gaining the courage and mustering up my faith, I went back to school. Not only did I get a degree, but I graduated with two degrees. So *yes, you can do it!* With the help of the Lord Jesus Christ, you *will make it!*

Another way out is by being obedient. If you are not obedient, you will remain in your situation. If you do not obey God's commands and His instructions for your life, you will be in places where your blessings, your healing, your deliverance, and your riches cannot reach you. Let me simplify this so that you understand what I am saying. If the Lord Jesus Christ called you to preach, do not run from it; obey Him and preach God's words.

If the Lord tells you to go to a new land, do all you can to go to that land, because by leaving your home land, the new land is where your blessings will be waiting for you. I have moved from job to job so many times that some people may think that I am not stable, but the Lord had planted me in various jobs for different reasons and purposes. In every job, I was able to accomplish something for the Lord, whether it was salvation, deliverance, healing, or just comforting someone who was in need.

Obedience to God is very important. When you obey God, you will be in a place where He wants to pour out all He has for you. It is not only God you should obey, but also your pastor. The head of the church, your pastor is totally responsible to God for you, so if he instructs you to do something, pray about it and obey.

Some people may not realize this, but our pastors must give an account to God when that day comes. If your pastor is not led of God and is doing any old thing in the pulpit, he has to account for leading his flock astray. Pastors who are called of God, directed by God, and anointed by God will lead their congregation in the direction that God wants them to go. When they give you a direction to take in life, obey it, follow it, and let the Lord have His way in your life. This tool of obedience is powerful. It is vital and it is mandatory if you want to find your way out of the many situations that satan has cornered you in.

Another way out is by paying your tithes. Yes, many Christians do not pay their tithes. I am telling you, if you do not pay your tithes, you will always have financial problems, you will always be in debt, and you will always be in want. I mentioned this in an earlier chapter. You must give back to the Lord one tenth of your first fruit (Malachi 3:8-10)—not the leftovers after you have paid the bills. Some people say you must pay yourself first, but I am telling you to pay the Lord first. I am living proof that by paying your tithes, the Lord will bless you bountifully. Since I was off work for over four years, whatever little I got, I still tithed from it, and my Father in Heaven has *always* blessed me.

Many years ago, Marilyn, a friend of mine, and I were walking and praying for the neighbourhood. I had a bill due that very day. All of a sudden, I looked on the ground and found a twenty dollar bill. Marilyn told me to take it and use it to pay the bill. We first looked to see if it had belonged to anyone, but there was no one in sight. I offered to split it with her, but she said no. That twenty dollar bill was used to pay my bill. My God provided for me and He will do the same for you, if you tithe, and if you give to others.

I am not only referring to money. I am talking about giving of your time, your talent and your knowledge. Always give your best and God's best will be given back to you, I promise.

The way out of satan's clutches, his lies, his deception, and his schemes are very simple. First, you accept Jesus Christ as your Saviour. Then you ask God to forgive you of your sins. After that, you give your all to Christ. When I say "give your all," I mean your all, your everything. Next you read God's words daily. You must pray daily and commit your ways to God daily. You must then obey God's words and obey your pastor. You must have faith, trusting in God when you cannot see him. Trust in God when you have nothing, when you cannot see how things will work out for you. Just tie a knot and hang on. Jesus Christ will always make a way out for you. Depend on God and know that our Father in Heaven will not leave you to suffer. Sometimes we may suffer, but this is not forever; Jesus Christ will always be in control if we let Him.

There are so many traps of the enemy. satan uses our friends, our loved ones, our bosses, our colleagues, and even our brethren in Christ to lead us away from God's plan and purpose for our lives. From today on, do not let satan have the victory anymore. The way out is simple, and it is sure, if you allow God total control of your life, if you obey Him, trust Him, pay your tithes, wait on God, and last but not least, depend on God. Do not have any doubts or fears. When our Father in Heaven says to us that He will do something in our lives, He will do it. Do not despair, but instead have faith and rely on Jesus Christ. Once you do that, the blessings, healing, deliverance, and all that God has for us will come pouring out to us. Praise be to God!

23
Victory in Every
Area of Our Lives

NO LONGER WILL WE BE LIVING A SILENT DEATH

Ten years ago, I had a dream. In the dream, the Lord asked me to write this book for Him. In that dream, I asked the Lord, "Why? Why do I need to write this book?" The Lord replied, "So that millions of people will be saved." I really did not know how to do it, where to begin, and what to write. When I began writing this book, I truly believed that it was only for women, but as the Lord directed, I touched not only on issues that plague women, but also on issues that involve men.

Our Father in Heaven has a plan and a purpose for these words. Our Father wants us to know Him, to love Him, and to live for Him. Our Father wants us to know the different techniques that satan uses to destroy our lives, our families, and our destinies. Our Father wants us to have victory in every area of our lives so that we will no longer be living a silent death.

Whenever I mentioned this book to my students, my family, and friends, they would ask about the meaning of the title, *The Silent Death*. The silent death means that there are ways in which one can die without realizing it. If you have a heart attack and die, this death is not silent. If you are in an accident and die, this death is not silent. A silent death results from things that are killing you silently without your knowledge. For example, spiritual things, physical things, emotional things, hereditary things, curses, and witchcraft.

Do not be naïve, thinking that there is no witchcraft and that there are no curses working in your life. Believe me, sometimes we curse ourselves by what we say to and about ourselves. Curses can be put upon you consciously and unconsciously, by your friends, your loved ones, your peers, or anyone who does not like you. It can be as simple as a *look*. Yes, a look. In Tobago, we call it a "bad eye."

So many of us get sick religiously, and when I say religiously, I mean almost at the same time every year, and we do not realize that this is satan's doing. My sister Claudette got sick and ended up in the hospital every year around the same month. This went on for a few years, until one day she was delivered from it and was set free. Since then, that sickness has never returned.

Some of us are debt-ridden and we do not seem to have any money at any given time. Some of us have what we call "leaking pockets." Nothing can stay with us. Many of us are constantly in debt, always having to be borrowing to pay off a credit card, a loan, a friend, or a family member. This is of the devil. This is not what God wants for us. The Bible tells us that God wants us to have and to have in abundance, so why should we lack?

Many of our young men and women are possessed by demons and do not even know it. So many young women find themselves confused—up today, down tomorrow. So many women cannot get married. Men are coming around, yet when it is time for the man to propose to them, they turn away. Many men and women are married to husbands and wives in the spiritual realm, and they don't know it.

The Lord God Almighty is saying to you right now that you are coming out. You are coming out of every trap that satan has planted for you. Today is your day that He, our Father in Heaven, is taking you out, and He is giving you the victory. There is only one thing that you need to do to come out and to have that victory, and that is to totally surrender your life to Jesus Christ, live for Him, obey Him, and let the Lord direct your path. Through Him, you will have the victory!

In John 14:3, the Lord Jesus Christ said that He is coming back. No one knows the day, the hour, or the second He will return, but we know He is coming back soon. We just have to be ready. Be ready to meet your Maker, be ready to give an account for your life, and be ready to live eternally with Him in Heaven.

The alternative to Heaven is Hell. That is your choice. If you do not accept Jesus Christ as your Lord and Saviour, if you do not live for Him, it means that you are living for the devil, and if you live for the devil, I guarantee that you will spend eternity in Hell with him. The choice is now yours to make.

In Matthew 11:28-29, Jesus said, *"Come unto me, all ye that labour and are heavy laden, and I will give you rest. Take my yoke upon you, and learn of me; for I am meek and lowly in heart: and ye shall find rest unto your souls."*

Jesus is telling us to come unto Him, all of you who are burdened with problems, sicknesses, poverty, curses, and with all

155

that satan has put on you. Jesus is saying to come unto Him and He will give you rest. He said to learn of Him in order to find rest unto your souls. This tells me that you and I will have everlasting peace, joy, and happiness if we live for Jesus.

It is my prayer for each one of you reading this book that your lives will be forever changed. It is my prayer that you will make the best decision in your life, and that is to follow Jesus, to accept Jesus Christ as your Lord and Saviour. It is also my prayer that when you make that step to live for Jesus, your life will never remain the same. I pray that you will be set free, delivered, blessed, highly favoured by God and by man, and that you will no longer be living a silent death. May God richly bless you and may your walk with Christ be a gratifying one!